LIFE IN THE SOVIET UNION:

A Report Card On Socialism

by

SVETOZAR PEJOVICH
Professor of Economics
and
Dean, Graduate School of Management
University of Dallas

Copyright © 1979 by The Fisher Institute

This edition has been produced as part of the
publishing program of The Fisher Institute.

ISBN: 0-933028-02-4 (paperback)
ISBN: 0-933028-03-2 (hardbound)
Library of Congress Catalogue Number: 79-55244
Printed in the United States of America
The Fisher Institute, 12810 Hillcrest Rd., Dallas, TX
75230

About the Author

Svetozar Pejovich is Dean of the Graduate School of Management, University of Dallas, and visiting professor of economics at Texas A&M University. He received his Ph.D in economics from Georgetown University, and his LL.B from the University of Belgrade. He has been a Research Fellow at Ohio University, and a Visiting Scholar at the Hoover Institution, Stanford University.

Dr. Pejovich is the author of *Market-Planned Economy of Yogoslavia; Economics of Property Rights* (with Eirik Furubotn); *Governmental Controls and the Free Market*; and a contributor to the *Journal of Economic Literature*, the *Journal of Law and Economics*, and other academic journals. He is also on the editorial board of the *Review of Social Economy*, and is the Chairman of the editorial board of The Fisher Institute.

TABLE OF CONTENTS

Foreword

Steve Pejovich has made important contributions to the scholar's understanding of communist economies. It is to be welcomed that he has taken up his pen to convey an understanding of the Soviet economy to a more general audience.

Fresh out of college in the summer of 1961, I went off to the Soviet Union as a participant in an exchange program. In my travels about that large country of diverse peoples, I was struck by the fact that goods and services that we take for granted in America were simply unobtainable in the Soviet Union. Ordinary, commonplace items such as toilet paper and chewing gum were simply not produced in the Soviet Union. There was no place to get a hamburger. Cars were few and living space crowded. The average Soviet citizen clearly did not have the living standard of an American college kid.

If our government bureaucrats were to apply the American definition of poverty to the Soviet Union, they would classify most of the Soviet population as poor. Yet, the country I saw could not be described as poverty-ridden. It was a more or less modern country, but one with a low standard of living — a country more modern than wealthy. Something seemed out of joint — sort of like taking an American city, jamming in more people but closing most of the stores and taking most of the goods off the shelves of those left open.

The Russians joked about their living standards. Their favorite was the "Adam and Eve" joke. The scene is the classroom, and the teacher goes down the list of inventions, asking the class who invented each one. The answer is always: "the Russians!" The teacher then goes down the list of famous people, asking their nationality, and again all are Russians. Finally, the teacher comes to Adam and Eve.

7

"Now class, what was the nationality of Adam and Eve?" "They were Russian," roars the class. "And how do we know they were Russian?" asks the teacher. Silence for a minute, then up goes a hand: "Because they had no clothes to wear, no roof over their heads, only an apple to eat between them, and they called it paradise!"

Although Russians would tell this joke and roar with laughter, they nevertheless seemed to expect that the day would come when Russia would be the most powerful country in the world.

Later in my studies as a graduate student and professor, I learned that the Russians' economic problem came from running the economy on ideological, rather than pragmatic, principles. The government had abolished private property and appointed managers to run the various enterprises. Instead of judging the managers' success according to whether or not they made a profit, the government rewarded managers according to whether they made their "gross output target," that is, say, 5,000 pairs of shoes or ten tons of nails.

The main result of replacing profit with a gross output target has been that Soviet managers can be successful even though their production is not very useful. For example, a manager whose target is a certain weight of nails will find it to his advantage to produce mainly large size nails and few small size ones. On the other hand, if his target is in terms of number, he will produce mainly small ones and few large ones. Whichever way it goes, the assortment of nails available is unsatisfactory from the standpoint of many users. Generalize this to all products, and you see why the Soviet consumer is worse off than he needs to be.

The Soviets are aware of this problem and have summed it up in a famous cartoon. A communist party official is pinning a medal, "Hero of the Soviet Union," on the manager of the nail factory for overfulfilling his target, and alongside are two cranes holding up one giant nail. But

Soviet rulers have not been able to do much about the problem, because they believe that a socialist government is inconsistent with private property and free markets.

The weaknesses of the Soviet economic system, however, have not prevented the Soviet government from assembling what is probably the mightiest military force that the world has ever seen. The Politburo doesn't have to worry about liberal Senators and Congressmen cutting the military budget in order to put more people on welfare. And military projects cannot be delayed by environmentalists bringing court actions. Whatever the defects of the Soviet system, it is very effective from the standpoint of allowing the rulers to exercise power.

Lenin based the Soviet system on power, and it has stayed there ever since. Listen to Lenin who laid it on the line: "The scientific concept of dictatorship means neither more nor less than unlimited power, resting directly on force, not limited by anything, not restricted by any laws, nor any absolute rules. Nothing else but that."

There is no evidence that Lenin's followers were shocked by this doctrine or that they discarded it upon his death. Rather, they took it for granted. For example, Grigori Pyatakov, who himself became a victim of the doctrine, recognized and approved it: "According to Lenin the Communist Party is based on the principle of coercion which doesn't recognize any limitations or inhibitions. And the central idea of his principle of boundless coercion is not coercion by itself but the absence of any limitation whatsoever — moral, political, and even physical."

Today this doctrine has a long tradition, and it has survived its practice by Stalin, Mao, and Pol Pot. The Hungarians ran up against it in 1956 and the Czechoslovakians in 1968. Dissidents in Russia run into it today when they appeal to the Soviet constitution and find that the party, instead, is supreme.

In the past we could cope with such an adversary because we were the world's number one military power and also had a stronger diplomatic position in international politics. Today this is no longer true, and it is not clear how our leaders will be able to avoid giving in to the Soviets on more and more issues.

In a speech to the U.S. Senate on June 23, 1978, Senator Orrin Hatch said: "It is remarkable that in spite of the universal bad name of the Soviet system, in spite of its heavy hand upon its own people and others, in spite of its many failures, it has essentially overcome an alliance of prosperous and free people who could have marshalled against it an overwhelming economic and military power."

If we have made a lot of miscalculations, it is because we have based our dealings with the Soviets more on hopes than on knowledge about the regime. In fact, for years the American public had very little accurate information about the Soviet Union. This was partly because Americans weren't very interested to know. But it was also because many of our intellectuals, whose job it was to inform us, were themselves socialists, and they were afraid that Soviet economic failures — to say nothing of the horrors of the purges and the death camps — would be taken as proof that American capitalism was better. Rather than tell the truth themselves, they denounced those who did. In his book, *The Great Terror,* the British historian and poet, Robert Conquest, describes some of their shameful attempts to silence and discredit people who had been in the camps or had told about the purges.

Because the Soviet system has so many faults, anyone who tells the truth about it risks being criticized on being critical. Consequently, many writers feel that they must demonstrate that they are "fair" by drawing a more or less even balance between the American and Soviet systems. "We have problems too" is an excuse offered by many for the far greater shortcomings of the Soviet system.

American society is very widely criticized today, not just in the Soviet Union but also in our own schools, movies, novels, news media, and politics. Criticism of America is so pervasive in our culture that it denies us a perspective on the rest of the world. If we are to survive as a nation, we must begin to view the rest of the world through the same critical eyes with which we view our own country.

Paul Craig Roberts
New York City
April 1979

Introduction

The purpose of this book is to provide a description of the Soviet social system. The Soviet Union is our major adversary. It has a marketable ideology that promises a sort of heaven on earth. However, there is a wide gap between the Soviet promises and the actual performance of the system. In practice, the Communist Party of the Soviet Union has completely succeeded in abolishing individual liberties. If there are economic pay-offs to the Soviet population we have yet to observe them. It is, then, important to describe for the American audience the actual life in the Soviet Union because it differs, and differs greatly, from the Soviet government's promises, aspirations and propaganda.

I believe this book presents an objective description of the lifestyle quality of the Soviet Union, which is perhaps the most oppressive and totalitarian state in the entire history of mankind.

It is important for us in the West to make a clear distinction between the Soviet ruling elite, which is bent on destroying us, and the Soviet people. The latter are warm, friendly and generous men and women. A Russian dissident, thoroughly disappointed with official attitudes of Western governments, told me: "If one day it should be your turn, then do not cry before your execution or your transport to a camp that you have been betrayed. You did want to be betrayed and did not listen to our warnings. Our conscience is clear."

In preparing this book for publication I have received financial assistance from the Fisher Institute, for which I am grateful. I also wish to thank the Institute for Contemporary Studies, Education Research Council of America, and *Modern Age* for their permission to use my previously published works. Finally, I wish to acknowledge the clerical assistance of Mary Beth Walsh.

PART I

HISTORY AND POLITICS
IN THE USSR

Chapter 1

People of the Soviet Union

The Soviet Union is the largest country in the world. It spreads over two continents, covers almost one-sixth of the world land surface, and is two and one-half times as large as the United States. The Soviet Union occupies more than half of Europe and about two-fifths of Asia. The total population in the Soviet Union is in excess of 250,000,000.

The Soviet Union or, more correctly, The Union of Soviet Socialist Republics (USSR), was known as the Russian Empire, or simply Russia, until the 1917 revolution. Even today it is not unusual for many people to call the Soviet Union by its traditional name, Russia.

The Soviet Union has more than one hundred nationality groups. National groups in the USSR have their own languages, tradition, customs, and culture. Unlike the USA, which is also rich with many national groups, the Soviet Union has never been called a "melting pot". National groups in the Soviet Union live in well-defined regions; even young people do not easily move away from their homes to other areas of the country. The Soviet people prefer to stick with their own kind.

The administrative division in the Soviet Union reflects the importance of ethnic origin. The country is divided into fifteen Union Republics, twenty Autonomous Republics, eight Autonomous Regions, and ten Districts. Each of these administrative units is named after the area's dominant national group. In addition, many national groups have no administrative area of their own, because they are too small.

There are fifteen major national groups in the Soviet Union. Those fifteen national groups account for about 90 percent of the total population, with Russians the dominant national group. Slavic people (Russians, Ukrainians, and Belorussians) make up more than three-fourths of the total population in the country. Table 1 lists all major national groups. Column three in Table 1 shows that a significant majority of each national group (except Armenians) lives in its own region. Table 2 shows the rates of population growth among the regions of the USSR. The average annual rate of increase in the country as a whole (1959-70) was 1.3 percent. The average rates for Europeans were generally below the USSR national average, while those for ethnic groups in Asia were above the national average.

Density of the Soviet population varies from one area of the country to another. In some parts of the Soviet Union, such as Moldavia and Ukraine, the number of people per square mile exceeds 200. Some parts of the country are virtually empty. Siberia covers about 43 percent of the USSR and has about five people per square mile.

According to the Soviet census of 1970, about 56 percent of the Soviet population lives in urban areas. However, the allocations of people between urban and rural areas varies from one region of the country to the other. Estonia has the highest percentage of people living in urban areas (65 percent), while Moldavia has the lowest percentage (32 percent). Table 3 shows the percentage of urban population in each Union Republic.

The Russian Orthodox Church was the official church in the Russian Empire before 1917. It is still the largest church in the Soviet Union, Slavs, Moldavians, and Georgians generally belong to the Orthodox church. Moslems are the second largest religious group in the Soviet Union. The Soviet government actively discourages people from attending church services. Many churches have been turned into anti-religious museums, or simply closed down. Yet one comes back from a visit to the Soviet Union convinced that its people are deeply religious. Unfortunately, the Soviet government does not publish statistics on church attendance.

Table 1
Nationality and Administrative
Status in the Soviet Union

Nationality	Numbers in U.S.S.R (In 000)	Percentage of Total Nationals in U.S.S.R. Living in their Republic
Russians	129,015	83.5
Ukrainians	40,753	86.6
Uzbeks	9,195	84.1
Belorussians	9,052	80.5
Kazakhs	5,299	78.5
Azerbydzhanian	4,380	86.2
Armenians	3,559	62.0
Georgians	3,245	96.5
Moldavians	2,698	85.4
Lithuanians	2,665	94.1
Tadzhiks	2,136	76.3
Turkmens	1,525	92.9
Kirgiz	1,452	88.5
Latvians	1,430	93.8
Estonians	1,007	91.9

Source: *Izvestiya,* April 17, 1971

Table 2
Average Annual Rates of
Population Growth

European U.S.S.R.		Asian U.S.S.R.	
Estonian	0.2	Armenian	2.3
Latvian	0.2	Kazakh	3.5
Ukrainian	0.8	Azerbydzhanian	3.7
Russian	1.1	Kirgiz	3.7
Belorussian	1.2	Tadzhik	3.9
Lithuanian	1.2	Turkmenian	3.9
Moldavian	1.8	Uzbek	3.9
		Georgian	1.7

Source: Frederick Leedy, "Demographic Trends in the USSR," in
Soviet Economic Prospects for the Seventies, Washington,
D.C.: Joint Economic Committee, Congress of the United
States, 1973, p. 450.

Table 3
Urbanization in the Union Republics

	Percentage of Urban Population
Russian	62
Ukraine	55
Belorussia	43
Uzbek	36
Kazakh	51
Georgia	48
Azerbaydzhan	50
Lithuanian	50
Moldavia	32
Latvia	62
Kirgiz	37
Tadzhikistan	37
Armenian	59
Turkmen	48
Estonia	65

Source: Frederick Leedy, *op.cit.,* p. 457

Chapter 2

History of Russia Before 1917

The Kievan State

The first Russian state was established in the ninth century around the city of Kiev. The Kievan state grew fast and reached its "golden era" in the 980-1050 period. Accomplishments of the first Russian state during that period were many. The first law code in Russia was enacted, Christianity became the state religion, and diplomatic relations were established with many European princes. The introduction of Christianity had profound social implications in the Kievan state. The Russian Orthodox Church quickly became a strong integrating force for all the different Slavic groups. It contributed to the development of the arts and literature in Russia. Artists and architects came from Europe to build and paint churches, Monks began to write books and chronicles in Slavic languages. The Russian Orthodox Church also became the depository of Russian tradition and culture.

The source of prosperity of the first Russian State was trade. As trade routes shifted to the Eastern Mediterranean (especially after the Crusades), the importance of Kiev as a major trading center declined. The decline of trade brought the golden era of the Kievan state to an end.

The Tartar's Rule

In 1228, Ghenghis-Kahn's Tartars defeated Russian princes in a major battle, which marked the beginning of the Tartar's conquest of Russia. When the Tartars entered Kiev in 1290, their conquest of Russia was completed. Russia became a part of the Tartar's empire called the Golden Horde. The Tartar Rule in Russia lasted two centuries until Prince Ivan III threw them out of Russia in 1480.

As rulers, Tartars were both lenient and cruel. They were cruel in reacting to rebellions against their rule, to unrest, and to any sign of disturbance in the country. They were lenient toward the people who accepted their rule. Tartars left local princes in charge of administering their regions. They did not try to impose their way of life and customs on the Russian people. Most significantly, Tartars left the Russian church free. They were primarily interested in receiving taxes and maintaining trade routes.

The Rise of Moscow

The first known mention of Moscow goes back to the mid-twelfth century when the city was a small military outpost. Unlike Kiev, Moscow prospered during the Tartar rule; its princes got wealthier and its territory grew larger. In 1330 the Russian Orthodox Church moved its seat to Moscow. From that time on, Moscow rather than Kiev became the center of religious life in Russia, and a depository of its culture and tradition.

The first Moscow ruler to be crowned "the Tzar of Russia" was Ivan IV (1547-1584). He is better known in history books as Ivan the Terrible. Ivan was a brutal, suspicious and, at times, almost insane ruler of Russia. However, his brutality was primarily directed toward land-owners (boyars).

Not all was bad in Russia during the years of Ivan the Terrible. He was a social reformer and quite a successful warrior. In the 1550's, Ivan enacted a law code which seated local representatives in administrative bodies of local governments and in courts. As a warrior, Ivan defeated Tartars, conquered Western Siberia, and reached the Caspian Sea.

In order to wage his wars, Ivan needed a permanent army. He created such an army by simply giving land to those Russians who promised to serve in the army for life. They had to buy their own weapons, horses, and support several foot soldiers. In exchange for soldiering they received land to support themselves. Professional soldiers could neither sell that land nor will it to their heirs. However, their sons were expected to step into their fathers' shoes and continue to serve in the army in exchange for the right to exploit the land. In this manner, Ivan created not only a professional army but also a new self-perpetuating elite.

It soon became obvious to Ivan that his professional soldiers were spending more time in the army than at home working their fields. A serious economic problem arose. To deal with the problem Ivan passed a series of laws which eventually tied peasants to the land as serfs. That is how serfdom became the economic foundation of Russian social life and military power.

The period of Russian history following Ivan's death in 1584, and extending until 1613 is referred to as the "time of troubles". In 1613 Michael Romanov was crowned as tzar. That event marked the beginning of the Romanov dynasty that ruled Russia until the 1917 revolution.

Russia under the Romanovs

During its rule of about 300 years, the Romanov dynasty produced eighteen tzars. Some Romanovs were outstanding rulers, while others were rather weak. However, they all had one common trait: each and every tzar from the Romanov dynasty believed in the autocracy; in his divine right to rule absolutely.

Peter I, Catherine II, Alexander I and Alexander II were among the most able tzars from the Romanov dynasty.

Peter I was the first important tzar in the Romanov dynasty. He was crowned, together with his half-brother Ivan V. in 1682. After many years of power struggles and intrigues, Peter finally secured the Russian throne for himself in 1696.

Peter wanted to westernize Russia. Thus, in 1698, he went on a long tour of Germany, Holland, England and Austria. Peter was deeply impressed by the industrial, military and cultural achievements of West European nations. In fact, he brought with him over 1,000 European technicians and scientists. They helped Peter build factories, ships and buildings. Peter also introduced European manners, clothing and other customs in his court. One of his major accomplishments was the construction of Russia's new capital, Petrograd (today's Leningrad). The city was built on one of the most difficult locations, and at a tremendous cost in money and human suffering.

In order to finance his development programs and wars, Peter raised taxes and passed laws that further tied serfs to the land they toiled. Militarily, Peter defeated Sweden and gained vast new territories, including the Kharelian peninsula and a part of Finland. For all his accomplishments Peter was named *Peter the Great.*

Catherine II was a German princess who assumed the throne when her husband, Peter III, died. Catherine was intelligent, educated and an attractive woman. She was a first class administrator and the first educated tzar of Russia. During her reign Russia became a major world power. Catherine patronized literary works, education and the theater. Actually, she wrote a few plays herself. Yet, she was, like all other tzars from the Romanov dynasty, an absolute ruler who tolerated no opposition.

Table 4
Russian Tzars from the House of Romanov

Michael	1613-1645
Alexis	1645-1676
Theodore III	1676-1682
Ivan V and Peter I	1682-1696
Peter I	1696-1725
Catherine I	1725-1727
Peter II	1727-1730
Anne	1730-1740
Ivan VI	1740-1741
Elizabeth	1741-1762
Peter III	1762
Catherine II	1762-1796
Paul I	1796-1801
Alexander I	1801-1825
Nicholas I	1825-1855
Alexander II	1855-1881
Alexander III	1881-1894
Nicholas II	1894-1917

Catherine imposed censorship on foreign literary works, banned Voltaire's books from Russia, and introduced repressive measures against the more liberal intellectuals. Catherine also showed little concern for the economic and social condition of the serfs. She was quick to put down revolts against her regime. For example, Pugachov, the leader of a major peasants' revolt was captured after several bloody battles, put in an iron cage for public display, and then executed.

Catherine streamlined the Empire's administration, divided the entire country into provinces, and appointed a governor for each province. The governor of a province reported directly to Catherine. Nobility and upper social classes elected their own representatives who assisted the governor. The result was that Catherine had better and more direct control over the affairs of her Empire, while higher social classes were drawn into local administration.

Catherine's years in Russia were also marked with a number of successful military ventures. New territories added to the Empire included Poland, Crimea, Georgia and territory along the Black Sea coast.

Alexander I was an able man who encouraged education, modernized state administration and streamlined Russian bureaucracy. Alexander's military achievements were considerable. He defeated Napoleon, and was the first Russian tzar to cross Europe and enter Paris at the head of his army. However, like all other Romanovs, Alexander repressed liberal intellectual ideas. In 1820, he banished the famous Russian poet Pushkin to a remote town of Ekaterinoslav.

Alexander II was a good Tzar. His major accomplishment was a partial emancipation of the serfs in 1861. More than 20,000,000 serfs became land owners in the early 1860's. Alexander lifted restrictions on foreign travel, relaxed censorship of literary works, and allowed many intellectuals (including Dostoevsky) to return from Siberia. He also improved the system of education in Russia, reformed the Russian courts, introduced (on a limited scale) trial by jury, and promoted self-government by local representatives in Russian cities and villages.

Yet Alexander II was unyielding on the subject of his right to rule absolutely, and he was impatient with those who criticized his rule and was quite severe with those who openly opposed him. He was assassinated in 1881.

Nicholas II was the last Russian tzar. His firm belief in the autocracy accelerated political activities in Russia. In 1895, the Socialist Revolutionary Party was organized and became the first Russian political party. The Social Democratic Workmen's Party was organized in 1898, and in 1903 the party split into two fractions: the Bolsheviks and the Mensheviks. Both fractions had the same objective: socialism. However, they disagreed on the means by which socialism should be brought to Russia. The Bolsheviks believed in a violent revolution, while the Mensheviks favored a slow evolution toward socialism. The Bolsheviks were led by Lenin.

Lenin was sent to Siberia for three years and then allowed to leave the country. Another Bolshevik, Stalin, was also sent to Siberia but he escaped from the camp and went to Finland.

A brief and quite unsuccessful war against Japan in 1904 on the one hand, and numerous street demonstrations against the autocracy on the other forced Nicholas to issue a decree in 1905. The October Manifesto, as this decree came to be called, promised to end the autocracy, establish the parliament (Duma), and grant many civil rights to the people of Russia.

In 1914 Nicholas II got an unexpected shot in the arm. The war against Germany temporarily united the Russian people (except the Bolsheviks) behind the throne. However, by 1915 military defeats and terrible losses suffered by Russian troops turned the tide against the tzar. Nicholas

II was forced to abdicate in 1916 in favor of a provisional government formed by Alexander Kerensky. Nicholas II and his family were sent to Tobolsk in Siberia and then to Sverdlovsk, primarily for safety reasons. By that time Lenin arrived in Petrograd (sent by Germans in a sealed train). On November 7, 1917, he and Trotsky led the Bolshevik troops against the Winter Palace. The provisional government surrendered to the Bolsheviks and its ministers were sent to jail. On July 18, 1918, Lenin ordered Nicholas II and his family be shot. The Soviet rule over the country began.

Chapter 3

The Soviet Rule

The Lenin Years

The November 1917 Revolution put the Communist Party in power. Yet it took Lenin several years to consolidate the Party's rule in Russia. He had to deal with the ongoing war, military interventions from outside, domestic opponents, and numerous social problems.

The Communist rule was unstable and threatened by powerful enemies. To survive, Lenin had to make peace with Germany. He entered into negotiations with Germany and signed a peace treaty in March 1918. This treaty, which is known as Brest-Litovsk treaty, was very unfavorable for the Russians. They agreed to withdraw from Finland, the Baltic States, and parts of the Ukraine and Caucasus. Lenin had no choice but to pay this price in order to stave off the German army. He also transferred the capital of Russia from Petrograd to Moscow, which is located deeper inside the country.

British, Japanese, American and Polish troops were sent to Russia to fight the Red Army. However, the objectives of the foreign interventionists were limited, their numbers inadequate, and they lacked decisive and daring leadership. This foreign intervention was never a serious threat to Lenin. The major threat came from inside Russia. In many regions of the country the Communist regime was opposed by regular troops and local population. The heaviest fighting took place in Siberia, Ukraine, and along the Don River where the Cossacks fiercely fought against the Red Army. Lenin called all his domestic opponents by the same name: The White Guard. However, those troops were a divided lot and the Red Army was able to deal with them one at a time. By 1922, all major pockets of resistance to the Communist rule were destroyed by the Red Army.

The Communist regime was also opposed by various segments of the Russian population. To deal with that kind of opposition Lenin organized the Soviet secret police and gave it virtually unlimited powers. Within a year, the Cheka, as the secret police was originally called, arrested and shot without trial about 8,000 people. According to Solzhenitsyn, the Cheka quickly outperformed the Romanovs, who permitted only 894 executions to be carried out from 1826-1905.

Once in power the Communist Party abolished private ownership of land, nationalized the banks and factories, and put most commercial establishments under governmental control. The right to vote was specifically denied to all merchants, clergy, and other "undesirable" elements, as they were called by the Party.

In March 1921, Lenin turned to the problem of his authority in the Party. He got the Party to decree that no individual member be permitted to criticize the Party leadership. This decree eliminated the last vestige of democracy from the Party and made it into a monolithic institution. The act said that decisions announced by the leadership must be accepted by all members of the Party and carried out without further debate. It changed the so-called "dictatorship of the proletariat" into the "dictatorship of the Party leadership."

The combination of war, terror and Lenin's social policies reduced Russia's economy to ruins. Industry, which was run by inexperienced members of the Party, came to a standstill. The ruble (Soviet currency) became worthless.

29

The peasants consumed what they could produce and refused to deliver food to the cities. The result was the famine of 1921-22, during which millions starved to death. Several revolts by peasants, workers, and even military units broke out. Lenin crushed them all by force.

Lenin had to do something to stave off a complete chaos. In 1921 he introduced a set of economic policies that came to be called the New Economic Policy, or NEP. NEP represented a major retreat for Lenin. It restored private property, and denationalized trade and small-scale industry. Managers of state-owned firms were instructed to maximize profits, while wages and salaries were set by market forces. This return to a sort of free enterprise economy lasted seven years. During that period Russia recovered from war and famine, and signs of general prosperity became quite obvious.

Khruschev's reference to the New Economic Policy is quite revealing. He said:

> *In essence, the New Economic Policy meant the restoration of private property and the revival of the middle class, including the Kulaks. The commercial element in our society was put firmly back on its feet. Naturally this was, to some extent, a retreat on the ideological front, but it helped us to recover from the effects of the Civil War. As soon as the NEP was instituted, the confusion and famine began to subside. The cities came back to life. Produce started to reappear in the market stalls, and prices fell.*[1]

It is remarkable to have Khruschev tell us that a return to capitalism was all that the country needed to get back on its feet.

---

[1]E. Crankshaw (ed.), *Khruschev Remembers*, Boston: Little, Brown & Co., 1970, p. 20.

Lenin suffered several heart attacks in the early 1920's, and they triggered a power struggle in the Soviet Union. Trotsky and Stalin were the leading contenders for Lenin's job. Trotsky was second only to Lenin in terms of prestige, but Stalin held the powerful job of General Secretary of the Party. Stalin was in position to appoint people to various party and government jobs. Of course, he was careful to fill the most sensitive positions with his followers. Shortly before his death in 1924 Lenin became apprehensive about Stalin and seemed to have wanted to replace him. However, Stalin was already too powerful to be fired as the General Secretary of the Party. After Lenin's death, the struggle for power began in earnest. Stalin emerged victorious to become the most powerful ruler of Russia, more powerful than any tzar had ever been.

The Stalin Years

Stalin exhibited a unique ability to out-maneuver his opponents, and by 1928 he was in complete control of the Communist Party. Of course that meant he was in full control of the Soviet government. However, it was not enough for Stalin to subordinate his opponents. He wanted to destroy them physically. And that is what he did in the 1930's when all his rivals, would-be rivals, could-be rivals and countless other people perished. He was in full control of the country by 1928, and became the absolute and much feared ruler by the mid-1930's.

The so-called Stalin Constitution was enacted in 1936. The basic principles stated in the Constitution were: "who does not work shall not eat", and "from each according to his ability and to each according to his contribution." The first principle established the legal obligation for each citizen to seek work. The second principle is quite interesting. It says that one's income must be related to his performance at work. That is, it is all right for incomes to be unequal as long as the performance at work is not equal!

31

The 1936 Constitution also recognized three social classes in the Soviet Union: workers, peasants, and the intelligentsia. Article 126 of the Constitution explicitly recognized the existence of social classes in the USSR: "The most active and conscious citizens in the ranks of the working class, the toiling peasantry, and the intelligentsia are voluntarily united in the Communist Party of the USSR."

In the late 1920's, Stalin abandoned the New Economic Policy (NEP) and began a drive to industrialize the country.

Economic planning was the primary vehicle through which Stalin hoped to industrialize the Soviet Union. In 1928, the First Five Year Plan was announced. It was followed by the Second Five Year Plan in 1933, the third in 1938, and a series of five year plans after the end of World War II. The most fundamental feature of each five year plan has been a strong emphasis on the development of heavy industry at the expense of both the Soviet consumer and Soviet agriculture. Soviet workers were severely punished for any sign of tardiness, shirking of responsibility or absenteeism.

Stalin's decision to collectivize Soviet peasants was a pragmatic one. Politically, the collectivization of land was an expedient way for Stalin to establish full control over Soviet peseants. Economically, the collectivization of land gave him full control over the distribution of food.

Peasants resisted collectivization by slaughtering animals and refusing to work their fields. The 1932-35 famine was the predictable outcome of Stalin's agricultural policies. Faced with an inadequate supply of food, the Soviet government opted to feed industrial workers at the expense of peasants. The government simply forced peasants to deliver to state warehouses as much food as they did before the famine. That is how and why the famine caused the most starvation in rural areas where millions of peasants perished.

By the end of the 1930's Stalin had to make some important policy decisions. He opted to make peace with Hitler. Stalin had no illusions that a permanent peace with Germany was possible. However, Stalin knew that his purges had decimated the Red Army, and he needed time to rebuild it. Stalin also wanted to establish a buffer zone between Germany and Russia in order to withstand the first wave of Germany's assault. Those two objectives, to gain time for the Red Army to prepare itself, and to establish a buffer zone between the German Army and Russian soil, explain Stalin's decision to sign the Soviet-German agreement in 1939. A secret protocol was attached to the Soviet-German treaty. It provided for the division of Poland between the Soviet Union and Germany. In effect, it permitted Stalin to move the Soviet border several hundred miles to the west. The treaty paved the way for Hitler to attack Poland and start the World War II. As for Stalin, at the price of letting Hitler invade Poland he had bought himself some time. The initial successes of the German Army forced Stalin to move the Russian frontier even further west by occupying the Baltic states and parts of Romania and Finland.

By the end of 1940 Stalin received intelligence reports about Hitler's decision to attack the Soviet Union. However he still needed time to equip and train the Red Army. For that reason he tried very hard until the last day to appease Hitler.

The war began on June 22, 1941. Within a few days the Red Army was in a full and disorderly retreat. On July 3, Stalin spoke to the Russian people. He said:

> *"Whenever the units of the Red Army are forced to retreat, all railway rolling stock must be driven away. The enemy must not be left a single engine, or a single railway truck, and not a pound of bread, nor a pint of oil. The Kolhozni-*

33

*ki must drive away all their livestock, hand their
grain reserves to the state organs for evacuation
in the rear. All valuable property whether grain,
fuel or non-ferrous metals, which cannot be
evacuated, must be destroyed."*

The effect of Stalin's speech on the Russian people
was enormous. A famous Russian writer, Simonov, said in
his novel, *The Living and the Dead*:

*"People loved him in different ways, whole-
heartedly, or with reservation; and some did not
like him at all. But nobody doubted his courage
and iron will. And now was the time when these
two qualities were needed more than anything
else in the man who stood at the head of a country
at war."*

The German plan was to capture Leningrad, Moscow
and Ukraine before the Russian winter set in. For the time
being it looked as if Hitler's objectives were to be attained.
The German advance into the Ukraine was swift and irre-
sistible. On September 17, the Germans entered Kiev and
their armour divisions surrounded four Russian armies.
Eventually, the Germans captured about 600,000 Soviet
soldiers. By the end of October, the Germans were within
fifty miles of Moscow. However, Stalin stayed in the city,
and on November 7 (the Revolution Day) he reviewed the
Red Army troops. The setting was quite dramatic and mo-
rale-boosting. The troops that marched by Stalin came
from the front, or were on the way to the front. Stalin spoke
to the troops about the "enemy at the gates of Moscow,"
and told them:

> *"The war you are waging is a war of liberation, a just war. May you be inspired in this war by the heroic figures of our great ancestors, Alexander Nevsky, Dimitri Donskoy, Minin and Pozharsky, Alexander Suvorov, Michael Kutozov. . ."*

This invocation of the great ancestors appealed to the Russian national pride and to their love for the country. Stalin's glorification of Russia had a tremendous psychological effect on the people's morale and their willingness to fight. Many historians claim that snow and bitter cold saved Moscow. That might be so, but it is also true that the Russians put up great resistance.

The German troops reached Leningrad late in August. As in Moscow, the Soviet resistance stiffened as the Germans approached the city. When Hitler realized that Leningrad could not be taken by force, he decided to surround it and starve its population. The German ring around Leningrad was so tight that the ciy's only contact with the mainland was via Lake Ladoga. When the lake froze the supplies were taken to Leningrad by trucks. This supply route was constantly bombed by the Germans, and Russians referred to this life-line of the city as the "corridor of death" and the "road of life".

By November food became very scarce in Leningrad. Children received 684 calories a day, office workers 581 calories, and hard laborers, engineers and other specialists were entitled to 1,087 calories. And even those incredibly low allowances were only irregularly available. It is believed that during the blockade of Leningrad close to 1,000,000 people died of starvation. The blockade was not lifted until the end of 1943.

By the Spring of 1942 Hitler began to gather his forces for a new offensive. But this time he did not have sufficient strength to attack on a wide front. The German offensive began on June 28 in the Ukraine. On July 28 the Germans captured Rostov, and the road to both Stalingrad in the east and the Caucasus in the south was laid open. Germans quickly penetrated the Caucasus in the south and reached Stalingrad in the east. Actually, they managed to take the city of Stalingrad except for a few isolated pockets of resistance. Then the German advance came to a standstill.

The Red Army began its first major offensive of the war on November 18, 1942. The purpose of the offensive was to cut off the German Sixth Army (about 300,000 men) in Stalingrad from the rear. The Sixth Army was one of the best German Armies. It refused to surrender and put up a great fight. The battle at Stalingrad lasted about two months and marked a major turning point in the war.

The battle destroyed the offensive capacity of the German Army; however, it did not destroy the German Army itself. From January 1943 to May 1945 the German Army was retreating but was not on the run. By the time the Red Army entered Berlin, Russian losses in human lives were stupendous (over 20,000,000), and the Soviet Union was totally devastated.

The end of the war found Soviet troops in Poland, the Baltic states, Hungary, Yugoslavia, Czechoslovakia, Bulgaria, Romania, East Germany and Austria. Communist governments were quickly installed in all those countries except Austria. In addition, Stalin incorporated the Baltic states and parts of Poland into the Soviet Union. He compensated the Poles by giving them an equal share of East German territory.

When the war ended Stalin had to face a difficult choice: either to maintain open and friendly relations with the West or to close down the frontiers. The first choice held economic advantages because the post-war economic situation in Russia was desperate. The second choice had a clear-cut political advantage; Stalin wanted to stabilize his hold over Eastern Europe. An "open door" policy toward the West would have made the job quite difficult. He opted for the second alternative and closed down the frontiers. The Cold War marked the remainder of Stalin's years until his death in 1953.

Post Stalin Years

Stalin's death in 1953 signaled the beginning of a power struggle among his lieutenants. The prize was huge and the candidates were many. Somewhat unexpectedly, Khruschev was able to outmaneuver all other candidates, and by 1956 he was clearly the top man in the Soviet Union. In fact, he felt secure enough to use the 20th Congress of the Communist Party (1956) to deliver a vicious attack on Stalin. Khruschev blamed Stalin for bloody purges, for labor camps, for mass murders, and for ignoring some convincing and reliable intelligence about German preparations for war with Russia. Of course Khruschev was part of Stalin's inner circle and had to be fully aware of everything that happened under Stalin. Yet he chose to attack his former master for the crimes they, in effect, committed together. There is a story that explains Khruschev's duplicity. During the speech in which he attacked Stalin someone from the audience is said to have shouted, "And where, Comrade Khruschev, were you when all this was going on?" Khruschev interrupted his speech and asked, "Will the comrade who said that please rise!" No one rose. Khruschev then said, "That, my dear comrades, is where I was."

Khruschev tired to eliminate some of Stalin's harshest policies. He stepped up the construction of apartments for workers, relaxed labor discipline by not prosecuting workers for tardiness, absenteeism and shirking. Khruschev also allowed thousands of inmates to leave labor camps and return to their homes. Artists and writers were also given a greater scope of freedom, resulting in some outstanding films (The Ballad of a Soldier) and literary works (Solzhenitsyn's *One Day in the Life of Ivan Denisovitch*). However, this so-called "period of relaxation;" in Soviet postwar history should be properly understood. Khruschev never relaxed the Party's control over the lives of Russian citizens.

In foreign affairs, Khruschev initiated the so-called policy of "peaceful coexistence". His definition of peaceful coexistence was quite simple: the West was not supposed to interfere in internal affairs of Socialist States, while the Socialist States are supposed to interfere in domestic affairs of Capitalist States. Khruschev saw peaceful coexistence as a vehicle for subverting the capitalist world. It was wrong for the West to interfere with the Soviet invasion of Hungary in 1956, but it was not wrong for the Soviet Union to interfere with the British intervention in Egypt in that same year.

It was Khruschev who built the Berlin Wall in 1961. His decision to build the wall was based on two considerations. First, the difference in the standard of living between West and East Berlin was quite obvious and terribly embarrassing to the Soviet Union. Second, the free access to West Berlin made it easy for East Germans to use the city as a relay station for their escape to the West. The rate at which East Germans were escaping to the West in the early 1960's was politically embarrassing to the Soviet Union and economically costly to East Germany. The Berlin Wall reduced this flow of people but at a high cost. The wall became a living, visible and unchallengable monument to oppression. In the West, only convicted prisoners are kept behind barbed wire.

In 1964, after a brief internal struggle for power, Khruschev was forced to retire and the top job in the Soviet Union was captured by Leonid Brezhnev. As of this writing, Brezhnev is still the Soviet leader.

Brezhnev turned out to be less tolerant of artists, writers and intellectuals in general. He arrested many intellectuals, imposed stricter controls over their works, and forced a few to leave the country. In general, historians are likely to judge the Brezhnev years as a partial return to Stalinism.

Chapter 4

Political and Social Structure in the U.S.S.R

The Communist Party

The Communist Party determines domestic and foreign objectives in the Soviet Union and monitors their implementation. The Party is the supreme decision-maker in Russia. It requires and gets total and unquestionable obedience from its members. Once the Party leadership makes a decision all party members must support it, and the government bureaucracy must execute it.

The Political Bureau of the Central Committee of the Communist Party of the Soviet Union (Politburo) is the most powerful body in the Party. It makes all important decisions that affect the life of each and every citizen in the Soviet Union. Those decisions are formally approved by the Central Committee of the Party, and then turned over to the Soviet bureaucracy for implementation.

In theory, local party units send their representatives to the Party Congress. At the Congress, which is supposed to be held at least every five years, the delegates elect the central Committee of the Party. The Central Committee is the highest governing body of the Party, and from among its members the Central Committee elects the Politburo; this is the highest executive organ of the Party.

In practice, members of the Politburo are the most powerful men in the Soviet Union. The Politburo is, in effect, a self-perpetuating elite from which one departs by death or in political disgrace. New members are appointed through personal connections. The Politburo decides whom the Party Congress should elect to the Central Committee. A slate of candidates proposed by the leadership is quickly and unanimously approved by Congress.

The late professor Warren Nutter summarized the basic workings of the Soviet system as follows:

> *It was Lenin's genius to recognize the importance of embellishing the Soviet Systems with all the trappings of democracy. If the people want a constitution, give them one, and even include the Bill of Rights. If they want a parliament, give them that, too. And a system of courts. If they want a federal system, create that myth as well. Above all, let them have elections, for the act of voting is what the common man most clearly associates with democracy. Give them all these, but make sure that they have no effect on how things are run.[2]*

The Party begins to influence Soviet citizens as early as they begin to walk. In elementary schools, children join the Pioneers. They attend lectures and meetings at which specially trained personnel teach them about freedom under communism and the exploitation of working people in the West. In their teens, children become eligible to join the Young Communist League. About forty percent of the eligible age group joins the League.

[2]G. W. Nutter, *The Strange World of Ivan Ivanov*, New York, World Publishing Co., 1968, p. 39.

41

When a Russian joins the labor force, he quickly learns that each and every organization is controlled by the Party. He also discovers that the best jobs are reserved for members of the Party and that Party members get promotions easier and faster. In general, a member of the Party finds it less difficult to move up the social ladder.

A Russian has incentives to become a member of the Communist Party. And those incentives are primarily economic rather than ideological. Yet the Party prefers not to have as its members those citizens who join it for economic gains. Ideally, the Party wants only dedicated, ideologically committed members. (However, that is easier said than done.) Even the most ardent believers do not seem to waste much time in turning their party membership into an economic advantage.

To become a member of the Party, a Russian must apply for membership at work; that is, at the place where he is best known. He must also have three sponsors who, in turn, are held responsible for his future behavior as a Party member. The Party membership in the mid-1970s was estimated at about 14,000,000.

The purpose of the Communist Party is to preserve and strengthen the control of the country by a small, self-perpetuating elite. The controlling element within the Party is the professional apparatus. This professional apparatus, along with the secret police, are the foundation upon which the Party's power over the entire country rests.

The Soviet Government

The Soviet government is the vehicle used by the Party to implement its decisions. The Soviet parliament is called the Supreme Soviet. It has two branches: the Soviet of the Union, and the Soviet of Nationalities. The former is similar to the House of Representatives in the U.S., while the latter is more like the Senate. Various national groups elect members of the Soviet Nationalities. Members of the Supreme Soviet are elected for a four-year term.

The Supreme Soviet elects the Chief of State (largely a ceremonial office), and the Soviet Council of Ministers, which is the executive branch of the Soviet government.

Union Republics and Autonomous Republics elect their own Supreme Soviets which are organized along the same line as the Supreme Soviet. At local levels, regions, districts and towns elect their own local Soviets.

The Supreme Soviet also appoints the Soviet Supreme Court judges, as does the Supreme Soviet of each republic. In addition there are regional, district, and town courts. The lowest court is the People's Court whose judges are appointed by local Soviets. Trial by jury does not exist in the Soviet Union. In lower courts judges are assisted by the so-called people's assessors.

The Supreme Soviet appoints the Chief Prosecutor for a seven-year term. He controls appointments of prosecutors at lower levels, and these lower courts prosecutors are responsible only to the Chief Prosecutor.

The organization of the Soviet government suggests that they have elections in the Soviet Union. However, when a Soviet citizen goes to vote he discovers that only one candidate is listed for each position to be filled. Of course, the voter can scratch the candidate's name off the list and write-in someone else's name. But who is to organize a write-in campaign? And who dares to lend his name to such a campaign? In addition, votes are counted by the Party representatives, and who is to ask for a recount? Those who fail to vote are considered to be unloyal citizens. That is why over 99 percent of voters cast their ballots.

No private groups or associations can be formed in the Soviet Union without explicit permission from the government. When people are asked to attend a meeting they know the Party wants them to formally approve that which has already been decided. Those approvals are given quickly and unanimously as one would have predicted. Soviet workers cannot complain about working conditions; books and articles are censored, and Soviet scientists and intellectuals are carefully monitored. There are only two major papers in the Soviet Union, Pravda (Truth) and Isvestia (News). Like all other journals and local papers they publish only approved articles that reflect the prevailing party line. There is no truth in the one, and little news in the other.

All Soviet citizens are issued identity cards which they must carry with them at all times. However, identity cards are not issued to members of collective farms. This policy of not issuing identity cards to Soviet farmers has an important consequence: It ties farmers to their collective farms in much the same way serfs were tied to medieval feuds. In the Soviet Union those people who do not possess identity cards cannot leave their residence for more than five days at a time. Through this measure, the Soviet government controls the flow of people between rural and urban areas. A farmer cannot quit his collective farm and move to another farm or to a different job. To do that he must have the permission of the local leadership. Even a city dweller is not allowed to move to another city unless he first obtains a job there or is admitted to a school. Those measures reduce the mobility of Soviet citizens. Operationally, they reduce the Party's cost of controlling the population.

What goes by the name of justice in the Soviet Union has little in common with the rule of law as we know it. Dissenting opinions are quite rare in that country, public decisions are never challenged, and political minorities do not exist. Thanks to the Party apparatus, the secret police and various forms of governmental controls, the Soviet government can assert that the socialist harmony of interest, a perfect concensus, has been achieved in Russia.

Social Classes in the Soviet Union

Soviet propaganda would never admit that social classes exist in the country. But they do.

Professor Katz prepared a valuable study on the Soviet social structure for the Joint Economic Committee of the U.S. Congress in 1973. He demonstrated the existence of six main social classes in terms of income differentials, education, privileges, and life styles. Income differentials in the U.S.S.R. are discussed later in this book. Figure 5 identifies those social classes.

Figure 5
Soviet Social Structure
I. The Elite (Upper Class)

1. Top leadership group
2. Cultural and scientific elite

II. Secondary Elite (Lower Upper Class)

1. Secondary, central and top provincial leaders
2. Higher level intelligentsia
3. Top private operators

III. Upper-Middle Class

1. Middle level bureaucrats
2. Top management and specialists in collective farms
3. Middle stratum in private sector
4. Workers' aristocracy
5. Middle level intelligentsia

IV. Middle Class

1. Petty bureaucrats
2. Lower level intelligentsia

3. Highly qualified workers
4. Secondary collective farm management and rich Kolhozniki
5. Top white collar employees
6. Private artisans

V. The Working Classes

1. Ordinary workers
2. Ordinary white collar employees
3. Middle level collective farmers
4. Lower groups in private sector (working on the subsidiary lots, low-earning artisans)

VI. The Poor Classes

1. Minimum wage laborers
2. Poorly paid white collar employees
3. Poor Collective farmers (in poor Kolkhozy)
4. Low income pensioners, families without breadwinners, etc.

Source: Leo Katz, "Sociological Studies on the Soviet Union" *Soviet Economic Prospects for the Seventies,* Washington, D.C. Joint Economic Committee, Congress of the United States, June 27, 1973, pp. 105-106.

The Soviet Educational System

The Soviet educational system is tightly controlled by the State and highly centralized. The Ministry of Education controls curriculum for all levels of education, approves textbooks, and supervises educational programs.

A Soviet youngster enters an elementary school at the age seven. The first eight years of schooling are compulsory; however, there is a movement in the U.S.S.R. to extend compulsory education through the tenth grade. About sixty percent of the eighth grade graduates enroll in general secondary schools, specialized secondary schools and vocational-technical schools. Others join collective farms or the unskilled industrial labor force.

General secondary schools are two-year schools. The Soviet high school student graduates upon completion of the tenth grade, rather than the twelfth grade as in the U.S. Upon completion of secondary education, the student can apply for admission to an institution of higher learning. Those who do not apply for admission in universities, and those who apply but are turned down, usually enroll in specialized secondary schools or enter the labor force. Since general secondary schools do not provide students with marketable skills, high school graduates who enter the labor force take evening or correspondence courses in various vocational programs. A high school student in the U.S.S.R. takes more mathematics, physical science, biology, and geography than a high school student in the United States, while an American student takes more courses in humanities and social sciences.

Upon completion of the eighth grade, soviet youngsters may enroll in specialized secondary schools. Admission to those schools is also open to high school graduates who wish to learn a marketable skill. Specialized secondary schools offer programs that last up to four years. Their graduates receive the equivalent of a general secondary education plus specialized technical training in nursing, engineering, technology and other technical and semi-professional skills. The major function of specialized secondary schools is to train skilled and semi-professional workers for the Soviet labor force.

Vocational-technical schools offer training in various occupations that last up to three years. They train young people for semi-skilled jobs in industry and agriculture. Academically, as well as in terms of social recognition, Vocational-technical schools are considered well below general and specialized secondary schools.

Institutions of higher education accept about one-fifth of the high school graduates. the number of students admitted and enrollments by field of study are determined by the overall economic plan.

How are students selected for admission to institutions of higher learning? The decision is supposed to be based on the student's performance in high school and on the college entrance examination. (And it usually is.) However, personal connections of the student's family are also quite important. Those students who are not admitted to Soviet institutions of higher learning enter the labor force, either directly or via specialized secondary schools.

Since 1956, higher education in the Soviet Union has been tuition free. In addition, most students receive stipends. The comparison is frequently made in the West between tuition-free education in the Soviet Union and rather costly education in the United States. The alleged difference in the cost of education is a false issue. In the Soviet Union higher education is both free and available only for a small and carefully selected group of high school graduates. In the United States, higher education is free for a select group of students who qualify for various scholarships. In that respect, there is no difference between the U.S.A. and Russia. However, higher education is *available* to all high school graduates in the United States at a price. The true comparison of the differences in the cost of education is between the American student who can get a university degree at a cost, and the Soviet student who cannot get a university degree at any cost. The American high school student who is not in the top 20' of his class has the same option as his Soviet counterpart: to join the labor force. But he also has an option that is not available to the Soviet student: to invest in his own education. In fact, total Soviet expenditures for education, divided by the population (i.e.

expenditures per capita) are only about 64 percent of the
U.S. average.

On November 13, 1974, the Washington Post published a very interesting story on the Soviet system of education. It quoted a graduate from the Moscow Institute of
International Relations:

> *The school was dominated by one goal, the
> one dream that was held up before all of us, the
> possibility of a trip abroad for practice work.*

> *It's a 'closed institute'. That means there is
> no public announcement inviting people to ap-
> ply. It doesn't appear on the list of ordinary col-
> leges. And when you apply you have to give them
> a 'kharakteristika' — a recommendation —
> from your local regional committee of the Kom-
> somol . . .*

> *If you look at the student body, you see that
> they are children of the privileged class . . . You
> can see whose children are admitted before the
> entrance exams when, for instance, generals
> come into the school wearing all their medals,
> and go right to the director's office. They come
> out after a while confident that their sons will be
> admitted . . .*

> *There was a strong caste system. Children
> of important people stick together; they don't
> mix with the rest. This extends to marriage. The
> son of the assistant dean of the institute, say,
> might marry the daughter of the director of the
> Bank for Foreign Trade. . .*

> *. . . And of course, that has nothing in com-
> mon with communism. Once after I graduated
> from the institute I was out with a girl who took
> me to the apartment of somebody she knew who*

was still a student there. There was a darkened room with 10 or 15 people sitting around. These were 'golden youth', as we called them. The apartment was very big and luxurious by Soviet standards.

Everybody chewed gum, sat there and listened to the record of "Jesus Christ, Superstar". That's sort of a typical scene: everything there was unavailable to an ordinary citizen — the chewing gum, the big apartment, the good foreign record. They already knew the record by heart; they sang along with the chorus.

Health Care In The Soviet Union

Free medical care is a central element in the Soviet welfare system. If a Russian gets sick he goes to a clinic where he is treated free of charge. The word "free" must be understood. It means that services are not paid for by those who consume (use) them, and at the time when they are consumed. The cost is born by *all* citizens via the taxes they pay. In fact, health expenditures for persons in the U.S.S.R. are about 34 percent of those in the U.S. Again, an article in the *Washington Post* pointed out that medical care in the Soviet Union is in fact quite expensive in terms of resources that are being wasted, and inadequate in terms of quality. The article titled, "Russia's Troubled 'Free' Medical Care", (November 10, 1974), said the following:

In all the state's facilities, health care is free for everyone. No Soviet family needed fear that an illness could bring financial difficulties.

But that is not the entire picture. 'Our free health care is very, very expensive," one woman complained in Moscow last spring after returning home from the hospital. She had been caring

*for a sick relative in an overcrowded ward—
bathing and feeding him and otherwise doing the
work Westerners expect nurses to do.*

*A Moscow surgeon said: "Like everything
else in Russia, medicine and medical care exist
on many levels." There is medicine in Russia
that is up to the best international standards.
There are many good doctors. But as far as free
medical care is concerned — well, I think it is the
scourge of Russia. . .*

*Say 50 people show up for office hours at a
neighborhood polyclinic. One doctor will handle
them all. He or she will have five hours to see
them. That's about six minutes per patient. And
the patient must undress and dress; he has to tell
the doctor what's bothering him; and the doctor
has to prescribe something and fill out the "hospital list," the document that excuses the patient
from work.*

*You know, a doctor's favorite kind of pa-
tient is a sales clerk from a shop, someone who
can help the doctor to buy something good.*

*And if there is such a thing as a good, seri-
ous doctor who thinks about the patients and
cares about them and who gives a patient 20 or
30 minutes of undivided attention, then there
will be long lines! People will start complaining
to the head doctor, and the head doctor will bawl
out this physician who is holding every one up . . .*

*A beginning physician gets 100 rubles a
month. (An average industrial worker in the Soviet Union makes 135). To earn 150 rubles —
about the most a physician can earn — the doctor must work a shift and a half, 12 hours a day.*

*Say he pays 12 rubles a month for his apart-
ment, another 7 rubles in transport. If he has a*

child attending kindergarten, that costs another 15 rubles a month. A doctor has to read certain papers and magazines which cost, say, 6 rubles a month. That's 40 rubles out of his salary right there.

Soviet doctors often prescribe drugs that they know are not generally available. A professor of pediatrics from a large provincial city discussed this problem:

"If a factory produces vitamins, say, or penicillin, and can make a certain amount of it above their planned target, then the factory will receive a bonus. It follows easily from there to decide to make the pills a little weaker than they should be, and to make a larger quantity of them — to produce above-Plan production . . . When we see that a medicine has no effect, we often say, 'that must be above-Plan production . . .' "

A Moscow doctor with experience in numerous hospitals said, "An overcrowded hospital is really something to see. Beds are jammed into the corridors, sometimes so tightly that there is no room to pass through. Beds are put next to the elevators, next to the dining rooms."

Like almost every aspect of Soviet life, medical care is reduced to vast tables of statistics. But the doctors interviewed for this article reported that medical statistics aren't always reliable. A professor of pediatrics elaborated:

"Sometimes the rates of incidence of certain diseases are artificially increased. Rheumatism, for example. About eight years ago it was suddenly discovered that rheumatism was five or six times more common in Russia than in England. How was this possible?"

What happened was they had created so-

called rheumatism centers in the big cities of the Soviet Union. The doctors working in these centers were told that the number of service personnel (nurses) would depend on the number of patients that came to see them. If they had, say, 100 patients they would get one nurse, 200 patients, two nurses, and so on. So the statistics began to rise.

Soviet Cities & Countryside

The population in the Soviet Union is almost evenly distributed between urban and rural areas. Moscow is the seat of the Soviet government, and its population is close to 8,000,000. In the center of Moscow stands the Kremlin, an ancient fortress and a symbol of Soviet power. The red brick wall around the Kremlin was built by Ivan III some five centuries ago. Just outside the wall is Lenin's tomb and a strikingly beautiful church, St. Basil Cathedral. The church was built by Ivan the Terrible who liked the church so much that, according to a Russia legend, he ordered the architect's eyes burned out in order to make sure that he would never design a more beautiful building for any one else.

The most affluent and powerful Russians live in downtown Moscow. Within minutes from the center are old residential areas that look much the same as they did in 1917. Further out are the Moscow suburbs, which are quite different from suburbia in the United States. Instead of residential homes with carefully tended lawns, Moscow is virtually surrounded with huge apartment buildings which house more than two million people. Those apartments look sturdy but are, in fact, poorly constructed. The typical apartment has two or three rooms. It is designed to conform to the official standard of nine quare meters (about 100 square feet) of housing space per person.

The city transit system is excellent. Busses, trolleys,

trains and the Moscow metro are clean, fast and inexpensive. In the mid-1970s, one could ride from one end of Moscow to another for an equivalent of seven cents.

Leningrad is the second largest city in the Soviet Union (about 4,000,000 inhabitants). It is a showplace of the old Russian grandeur. In Leningrad you feel like you are in a beautiful European city. The people of Leningrad are friendly, sophisticated and more relaxed than Moscowites.

Smaller cities in Russia have few paved streets. The homes are mostly small cottages accommodating several families. The shortage of housing is quite acute because small cities have a lower priority for funds. It is not unusual to see two or three TV antennae on the roof of what a Westerner would consider to be a one-family dwelling. They indicate the number of families sharing the house.

The Russian village, with its high birth rate, has been for centuries a source of the supply of labor for Soviet industry. Russian villages all look alike. The homes are small, plumbing is nonexistent, and sanitary facilities are primitive. The family laundry is often done at a nearby creek. The center of the village usually has a general store, a church that is used as a storehouse, a school, a library, and the collective farm's headquarters. The life of a villager is difficult and dull. As pointed out earlier, the Soviet government had to deprive peasants of identity cards in order to keep them in their villages.

What are the Russians like? Under Stalin it was quite dangerous for an ordinary Russian to be seen with a foreigner. Even today, when contacts with foreigners are more numerous and less dangerous, we know very little about the life of an average Russian. Our contacts are mostly limited to those Russians who belong to the ruling elite and upper social strata. The behavior of those Russians does not reflect the "likes" and "dislikes" of an ordinary man. They know that they are being watched, and tend to be courteous, reserved, and somewhat cold.

To learn what the average Russians are like one must avoid officials, guided tours and good restaurants. A great deal can be learned about Russians by walking side streets at night, eating in small restaurants, watching children at play in parks and travelling in slow trains. The picture that emerges is one of wonderful, warmhearted and very friendly people. Perhaps the most striking characteristic of the Soviet people is their appreciation of history. In front of every museum in the USSR one finds long lines of ordinary people who wait for hours to see an event or relics that commemorate their past. One also discovers that Russians are avid readers. The books they read are usually about wars or other historical events.

Children in the Soviet Union are well mannered and courteous. They invariably show respect for older people. They are also dressed better than their parents. Even in villages, children's clothes are of poor quality but clean and pressed.

Housing in the Soviet Union

The housing situation is quite critical in the Soviet Union. The quality of buildings is poor, and the supply of housing units is grossly inadequate. The late G. Warren Nutter used to say that the Soviets had perfected the art of constructing old buildings from scratch. Some estimates suggest that about half of all housing in the Soviet Union is without running water or sewerage. In the mid-1970s, living space per person was about 11 square meters (approximately 120 feet) which is about half that available in Western Europe[3] and little more than a fourth that provided in the U.S.A. Yury Krotov, a Soviet defector, described his Moscow apartment, which contained 100 square feet of

[3]W. S. Smith, "Housing in the Soviet Union", in *Soviet Economic Prospects for the Seventies*, Washington, D.C. Joint Economic Committee, Congress of the U.S., 1973, p. 405.

living space, as follows:

> *Our apartment contained eleven rooms. It had one kitchen with eight gas-rings, three bells (one general, and two individual), a telephone in the corridor which was in constant use, a bath, and a lavatory, which only the fastest were able to get to in the morning (the others stopped in at the public lavatories on their way to work). There were eighteen people in the apartment, besides myself. Seven families, seven meters for electricity, seven tables and cupboards in the kitchen, and seven launderings a month, since none of my neighbors used the state laundries. This was not because they did not like them, but because they were economizing. There was not a single washing machine in the apartment; we had never even heard of a clothes dryer. But there were three television sets and two radios. Furthermore, all eighteen people ate at home. They never went to even the cheapest cafeteria, much less a restaurant. Again, it was because of the expense . . .* [4]

Housing units in the Soviet Union are built by the government, cooperatives, and the private sector. The government housing program is financed from administrative budgets and the firms' own funds, which is also the government money. The share of housing financed by the government amounts to about two-thirds of the housing space produced annually in the Soviet Union. Monthly rentals are not expected to recover the cost of investment. Moreover, rental payments are estimated to cover only about one-third of the cost of maintenance. For example, the

---

[4]Y. Krotkov, *The Angry Exile*, London: William, Heinemann, 1967, pp. 125-127.

rental charge averaged about 1.5 rubles per square meter in 1972, while maintenance costs averages about 4 rubles per square meter[5]

Cooperatives are association of Soviet citizens who are "... permanent residents of a given locality, and in need of improving conditions."[6] Members of a cooperative have to put down as much as 40 percent of the total cost and pay the balance over twenty years. In addition, the members have to pay for the maintenance of the building. The individual who invests in cooperative housing does not become an owner of the apartment. He has the right to live in it, but the cooperative owns the building.

Privately built homes are usually found in smaller cities and rural areas. Those homes are small, often built without plumbing, and located on unpaved streets.

[5]W. S. Smith, op. cit., p. 412

[6]*Ibid*, p. 412.

PART II
THE SOVIET ECONOMY

Is socialism a workable social system? Is it possible for an economic system to operate efficiently without free markets and private ownership of capital and land? To assert that the Soviet economic system cannot work is readily refuted by empirical evidence. The Soviet economy has survived quite a few decades.

It is generally wrong to assume that a country's economy must go bankrupt because its economic system is inefficient. For example, there are two ways to go from New York to Los Angeles; I can fly in a jet or I can ride on a horse. Both methods will get me to Los Angeles. So to say that the Soviet economy is inefficient does not mean that it cannot work. The real question in discussing the Soviet economic system is *how well does the system work?* Could it work more efficiently?

A student of Soviet economics discovers a puzzling contradiction. He learns that the Soviet economy has had high rates of economic growth, maintained stable prices, and made some important technical advances. The student also learns that the Soviet economy is ridden with waste and inefficiencies. An intelligent person would reject some ready-made and generally meaningless explanations of this contradiction and raise a fundamental economic question: Is the analysis capable of explaining how and why the Soviet economy can generate economic advances in an environment that is pregnant with inefficiences? The answer to this question is in the affirmative and will be specifically explained in our discussion of the Soviet firm.

The analysis of the Soviet economy in the rest of this book will concentrate on several key issues: economic growth, the system of economic planning, the economic position of the Soviet consumer, Soviet agriculture, and the Soviet firm.

Chapter 5

Soviet Economic Growth

Economic growth is a rate of change in gross national product (GNP) from one year to another. It measures the increase in the *value of input* that is available to the community. The rate of growth can be expressed in either current prices or constant prices. The latter eliminates the effects of inflation on the value of output. The rate of growth can also be adjusted for the population growth. For example, if the rate of economic growth in a given year was five percent while the population grew at two percent, the rate of growth *per person* during that period was only three percent.

An increasing flow of goods and services contributes to the nation's well-being. The relevant question is: what are the sources of economic growth? The following factors have been considered as sources of growth: The availability of resources, the saving-investment relationship, and innovation.

The Supply of Resources

Empirical evidence does not support the contention that the availability of resources assures a high rate of economic growth. Much depends on how efficiently the resources are used. Japan has obviously done a better job of using its resources than India. Germany has used its U.S. foreign aid more efficiently than African and Asian countries. The Soviet Union is rich in resources but it is having a rather difficult time to clothe, feed and house its people.

One point must be clearly understood. Resources are *created*: they are not just discovered. Things become resources only after somebody discovers that they can be converted into useful goods and after he (or somebody else) proceeds to convert them into useful products by efficiently organized economic activity. To say that the United States has large supplies of resources explains nothing. Those resources were available to the Indians for centuries, but the Indians were poor. The midwest prairies and Texas plains were uninviting and underdeveloped until the incentive effects of a private-property, free-market system transformed them into the most affluent parts of the world.

Savings and Investment

The growth of output in a country is related to the growth of its stock of capital. If the marginal productivity of capital is 20 percent, then 1,000 invested in the production of capital goods should be expected to increase the annual flow of output by 200. Thus, the rate of growth depends on the *supply of investable funds* on the one hand, and the *productivity of capital goods* on the other. The reliance on investment has been the major source of economic growth in the Soviet Union.

Clearly, economic growth is not a free good. That is, it can be purchased at a cost. The cost of growth is the value of current consumption that is being given up. That is, *saving* is the major source of investable funds. Every dollar the community saves will increase its wealth and future incomes. To achieve this increment in future incomes, the community must sacrifice $1 worth of goods now.

Since a reduction in current consumption in favor of future consumption is a major source of growth, the growth-oriented government in the USSR finds it desirable to supplement the community voluntary savings with forced savings (e.g. *via* taxation of consumption). Suppose that the gross national product is $1,000, productivity of capital is 25 percent, and the amount of voluntary savings is $200. The increment in the gross national product is then $50 (200 x .25), and the rate of growth is 5 percent. If the Soviet government wants the gross national product to grow at 7.5 percent, it would be necessary to increase investment by an additional $100. The excess investment outlays must then be financed with the funds which were *not* made available via voluntary savings. The government must extract additional savings from the community. That is, the government must reduce private consumption by $100 in order to make $100 worth of resources available for additional investment. Since the community has not provided those additional funds voluntarily, the rate of growth beyond 5 percent makes the community worse off. The rate of growth preferred by the community is revealed by its voluntary savings. That is why a high rate of growth does not necessarily mean that the economy is doing well.

Productivity of investment is subject to the law of diminishing returns. Each increase in the rate of investment yields an addition to the total output. As the rate of investment per period of time increases, the rate of growth will increase at a decreasing rate and eventually stagnate.

Innovation

Innovation is the major source of economic development in a free market economy. Innovation means doing something that has not been done before. It could mean the development of new sources of supply, the introduction of a new good, the opening up of a new market, or the introduction of a new method of production. In any case, the act of innovation means an increase in the community's welfare via a more efficient use of resources.

The man who injects something essentially new into the flow of economic life presents the community with a choice between the old and a new use of resources. He enlarges the community's set of opportunity choices. The voluntary acceptance of the new alternative indicates that the community considers it superior to some old ones. Otherwise, the innovation would have failed. While an increase in the rate of investment contributes to future outputs by a reduction in current consumption, a successful innovation increases the community's welfare by adding to its range of choices. Moreover, the act of innovation does not have to affect the allocation of resources between present and future consumption.

The major difference between the effects of investment and innovation on economic growth can now readily be seen. The former leads to an increase in future outputs via a combination of voluntary and involuntary sacrifice of current consumption. The voluntary sacrifice of current consumption represents a desired adjustment in the community's pattern of consumption through time. The involuntary savings (forced savings) show the desired adjustment of the community's pattern of consumption through time. The involuntary savings (forced savings) show what a desired adjustment of the community's pattern of consumption should be in the opinion of the ruling elite. Innovation, on the other hand, increases the community's set of opportunity choices. This is brought about by the innovator, a person who knowingly and willingly accepts the risk of having his or her suggestion rejected by the community. The resulting change in the innovator's wealth (i.e., his or her profits) can, therefore, be treated as a social reward for making the community better off.

Since the flow of innovation cannot be planned or ordered in advance, the essential problem of relying on innovation as a major source of economic growth is one of creating an environment conducive for carrying out innovating activities. The right of ownership and contractual freedom are essential requirements for maximizing the flow of potential innovations. Both requirements are nonexistent in the Soviet Union. That is why investment in capital goods is a major source of economic growth in the USSR.

Indeed, gross investment has been the major source of economic growth in the USSR. Gross investment as a share of Gross National Product has increased from 24 percent in 1960 to 27 percent in 1970, and 29 percent in the mid-1970s. In comparison, gross investment as a share of Gross National Product in the United has remained at about 17-18 percent during the same period.

Our discussion of economic growth explains both the rising rate of investment in the Soviet Union during 1960-1970s period, and the accompanying decline in the growth rates.

Soviet growth rates declined during this period (in spite of higher investments) because the government couldn't depress current consumption by as much as was necessary in order to offset the law of diminishing returns. Table 6 shows annual rates of growth in the Soviet Union. Declining growth rates in the USSR have been associated with a rising rate of capital formation. In the United States, the growth rate (3 percent), and the rate of investment (17-18 percent of GNP), have been relatively stable during the 1964-75 period. I believe the comparison between growth rate and capital formation in these two countries is quite suggestive. The rate of economic growth in the USSR is achieved at a high cost to the Soviet consumer in terms of his current consumption; or more correctly, in terms of his preferred life-time pattern of consumption. On the other hand, the flow of innovation is a major source of economic growth in the United States.

Table 6
U.S.S.R.: Annual Rates of Growth

Year	Growth Rates
1951-60	5.8
1961-70	5.1
1971-75	3.7
1976	3.7

Source: *Allocations of Resources in the Soviet Union and China-1977,* Joint Economic Committee, Congress of the United States, part 3, p. 3.

Chapter 6

The System of Economic Planning
In The U.S.S.R.[7]

The Soviet ruling elite is growth oriented and determined to control the size and composition of national output. Given those objectives, the ruling group imposes strict governmental controls over the allocation and use of resources by basic productive units (firms, farms, institutes).

The Soviet government allocates resources and assigns productive targets to all industries and firms in the economy. All decisions concerning the level and character of the economy flow from the top leadership through various bureaucratic channels down to productive units. The sum total of these administrative orders is the economic plan.

The central Soviet planning agency, Gosplan, is an executive agency. It provides economic and technical solutions for decisions, directives and instructions issued by the top leadership in the Politburo. Operationally, the Politburo controls Gosplan through the administrative sections of the Party's Central Committee concerned with economic matters. In addition, Gosplan is also supervised by the Council of Ministers, the highest executive agency of the Soviet Government. But since the director of Gosplan is also a vice-chairman in the Council of Ministers, the deci-

---

[7]This Chapter is based on the Author's paper, "The End of Planning" published in *The Politics of Planning*, San Francisco Institute for Contemporary Studies, 1976.

sion-making powers wielded by Gosplan are fewer than one might expect for an institution responsible for economic planning. In the Soviet hierarchy of political and economic institutions, Gosplan is restricted to technical expertise in the preparation, modification, and execution of the plan. It prepares both current (annual) and long-range plans, sets and controls prices, and rations the use of raw materials and intermediary goods (the goods in process).

The long-range plan is a blueprint of the economic program for a five-year period. It identifies a number of targets that economic units will be expected to attain. G. Warren Nutter defined the long-range plan as a hazy vision of things that it would be nice to have — something for the planners to shoot at and the ministry of propaganda to shout about. The current annual plan is an operational document that specifies production assignments, sources of supplies, and delivery dates for economic units.

The Party leadership sets objectives for the economy. Gosplan then translates those objectives into production targets for business firms, state farms, and collective farms. It sends preliminary targets via bureaucratic channels to various regions, industries and firms. Those preliminary figures are related to the past performance of productive units, new capacities, new priorities, changes in productivity and so on. Productive units must then send back their comments and suggestions. Of course, they tend to understate what they can do and overstate what they need. In short, Soviet planners and the managers of productive units meet with fixed bayonets.

The most pressing problem facing Gosplan is that production targets must not, in the aggregate, exceed the economy's productive capacity. The target plans must be balanced, and balancing creates an enormous problem for Soviet planners. For example, the machine tool industry is turning out about 125,000 products. Thus, in that industry alone, Soviet planners have to take into consideration about 15,000,000,000 possible relationships.

In the Soviet's centrally-planned economy, each firm's output depends on the availability of raw materials and intermediary goods produced by other firms. Thus, the economic plan must prescribe not only outputs of individual firms, but also the allocation of inputs. Assuring a regular and adequate flow of raw materials and intermediary goods to productive units is thus the central problem in the Soviet system of economic planning. And the supply plan is therefore the core of the Soviet economic plan.

In a market economy, business firms bid for supplies in the market. To allow firms to do the same in a planned economy could easily disturb the plan's objective and frustrate the will of the ruling elite. Thus, economic planning must eventually lead to the planning of supplies. In the Soviet Union, Gosplan controls the allocation of about 2,000 inputs, while various ministries and lower level bureaucracies allocate another 38,000 inputs. In total, the Soviet bureaucracy thus controls the allocation and use of about 40,000 inputs.

Sizeable bureaucracies have been established to administer supply planning. In theory, firms are told what inputs they will get, in what quantities, from whom and when to expect deliveries. In practice, supplies arrive late or never. They also come in wrong quantities and specifications. The result is that even a small deviation from the supply plan can easily cause a chain-reaction throughout the system. Suppose that a firm that produces screws and bolts fails to deliver them on time to other firms. The rate of output of those firms is immediately affected. And in turn, enterprises that depend on those firms' output then become affected. And so on.

So-called *material balances* play a key role in preparation of the supply plan. Soviet planners draw material balances for all products in physical units. The balance for each input shows its sources (inventory, current production, imports) and uses (inventory, current production, exports). On the basis of material balances and production targets, the supply plan determines the allocation of inputs to individual enterprises. Again, several layers of bureaucracy are involved in this process.

Business enterprises provide information to their administrative supervisors about technical coefficients that relate inputs to outputs. On the basis of those reported production functions of business firms, past performances of enterprises, some expected (planned) changes in productivity, and the knowledge that the managers of business firms never tell the whole truth, the Soviet planning bureaucracy develops the supply plan. The final figures are far from perfect, however, because the number of interdependent relationships that must be integrated into the plan is too great. Soviet planners can neither generate information about those relationships nor produce a computer to handle them all.

Professor Vaughn, in her penetrating essay on "Economic Calculation under Socialism," wrote:

> *Considerations of the process by which equilibrium is approached, the effect of uncertainty... considerations of what constitutes economic information and to whom it is available are ... sufficient to guarantee that an economic order resulting from conscious planning ... will be far different from the one envisioned by the planners.*
>
> *The real problem is to show how the information necessary for rational decision making which exists in the minds of millions of separate individuals can be transmitted to appropriate decision makers in such a way as to permit an orderly economy to emerge. The information that individuals use to guide their economic activity is vast, detailed and necessarily incom-*

plete ... such information is not given, but is subject of continuous discovery.

The job of correcting even a minor mistake in the plan is enormous. Suppose that planners detect that the production of screws is lagging behind the planned rate. Clearly, they must increase the allocation of coal, steel, iron, and so on to the firms producing screws. But to do that, they must reduce the allocation of coal, steel, iron, and so on to other firms. And they must then reduce the planned rate of output of these firms, as well as other firms that depend on them, and on and on. Every time a mistake in the plan is noticed, the supply and production plans for a number of industries must be revised. As an example, the 1961 plan for the Tartar Autonomous Republic was modified five hundred times. When these modifications occur, in effect, the plan is constantly revised and brought in line with the business firms' actual performance. Thus, in the course of the year, the plan and the economy's actual performance eventually converge, and at the end of each year the Soviet press can therefore honestly report that the annual plan has been fulfilled.

For example, the average rate of growth of total industrial output was set at about 8 percent per year in the 1971-75 plan. The actual rate of growth in 1971 and 1972 fell off to 6.1 and 5.4 respectively. Then, the Soviet government simply reduced the planned rate of growth to 5.8 percent per year.

It is clear that revisions and adjustments in the plan must result in lower output targets for many firms and industries. To take care of this, the ruling elite designates certain sectors of the economy as low-priority areas. And for this purpose consumer goods industries have consistently been assigned the task of bearing the cost of miscalculations, inadequacies and inconsistencies in the plan. Put another way, centrally-planned systems need a buffer to absorb mistakes in the plans. In the Soviet Union, the consumer serves that function.

The Soviet government is genuinely interested in improving the performance of the nation's economy within a given set of political constraints. To this end, the government has consistently relied on material incentives to reward the managers and employees of business enterprises for meeting and exceeding their planned targets. The so-called *success indicators* (gross value of output, labor productivity, cost per unit of output) are used to evaluate the performance of business enterprises. In effect, success indicators are simply a form of control over the management of firms. They evaluate each firm's performance in relation to its plan. The number of success indicators has changed frequently. From as many as 40 indicators in the 1950s, the number was reduces to 9 in the 1960s, and raised to about 15 in the 1970s.

For at least two reasons, Soviet planners must closely monitor the performance of productive units. First, to make adjustments in the plan, Soviet planners must have information about its shortcomings, miscalculations, bottlenecks, supply problems, and so on. Second, planning without control could easily frustrate the Party's objectives. It would be like planning a candy-free diet for a six-year-old. Unless his parents take on the cost of controlling him, the boy's real diet will almost certainly frustrate the parents' "plan." One important device for monitoring the execution of the plan in the Soviet Union is the financial plan.

The Soviet firm's financial plan is the monetary equivalent of its production plan. Like the budget of a government bureau in the U.S., the financial plan of the Soviet firm identifies its receipts and expenditures by categories. Unlike the budget, it specifies both the firm's contractual partners and the terms of exchange. Suppose that a firm is told to produce 1,000 television sets per month and deliver them to specified retail stores at $100 each. Assume also that the firm's supply plan allocates to it 1,000 wooden boxes at $30 each, 10,000 screws at 25 cents each, $20,000 for wages, and a total of $40,000 for other inputs. The firm's planned revenue is $100,000, planned expenditures are $92,500, and planned profits (inclusive of turnover tax) are $7,500. Depending on the Party's priorities, the firm's planned receipts are equal to, greater than, or less than its planned expenditures. In our case, the surplus is $7,500, and it is used to subsidize other (higher-priority) firms and governmental activities.

All transactions of Soviet business firms are done through the bank, which transfers funds from one account to another. Because all payments must be made through the bank, the bank checks those payments against the firm's financial plan. The Soviet firm cannot withdraw cash to make payments to its contractual partners. Such payments would escape the planners' control over the firm's transactions and could interfere with fulfillment of the plan by other firms.

The financial plan thus serves two major functions. By controlling the flow of receipts and expenditures of business firms, the bank can detect miscalculations and bottlenecks in the plan, and alert the appropriate planning bureaus. Also, the bank serves the function of a watchdog. Any deviation from the plan at a firm's level could easily interfere with the leadership's objectives for the economy. Suppose that the manager of a firm uses more resources than he is supposed to, or that he produces a different assortment of goods. His actions will have a chain reaction throughout the system. If he uses more resources than he was supposed to, shortages of those resources will appear elsewhere and affect the fulfillment of the plan. If he produces a wrong assortment of goods, business firms which use his output as intermediary goods will be affected. It is then important to the government to make sure that the firm's managers do as they are told. The financial plan helps the state facilitate this type of control over enterprises. It also helps the government reduce, if not eliminate, deviations from the plan by business firms.

The financial plan could, under some circumstances, complicate the planners' job. Suppose that the price of screws rose from 25 cents to 35 cents. The firm's budget of $2,500 would then not be sufficient to purchase 10,000 screws. The firm's payment of $2,500 to its suppliers would give no assurance to the bank that the firm has received all the screws it needs to produce 1,000 television sets. The planners' cost of monitoring the execution of the plan would therefore increase.

Because stable relative prices are important to Soviet planners, planners *make* them stable by administrative decisions. With few exceptions, most prices in the Soviet Union are set by the government and are rarely changed. Soviet prices are not meant to determine *who gets what* and *who does what*. No Soviet citizen can raise his money offer to bid a good away from other claimants. Market prices are scarcity prices. They are the outcomes of continuous interactions of utility-seeking individuals; they are a means by which individual preferences are transmitted to decision-makers. To replace market prices as a method of coordinating human actions is like giving up flying for walking.

Administratively controlled prices are by definition stable prices. Does that mean the absence of inflation in the U.S.S.R.? Not at all. It only means that inflationary pressures reveal themselves differently in the United States than in the Soviet Union.

The Soviet government often says that there is no inflation in Russia. Of course, inflation as we know it is not a feature of the Soviet system. In our system we define inflation as an increase in the average price level. In Russia all prices are set by the government, and the government has only to refuse to change them and there will be no inflation. But is it true that they have no inflation in the Soviet Union? Let us see.

Suppose that everybody in the United States receives an extra $100. What are the prople going to do with that extra income? They will spend at least some of it. Suppose that, among other things, they want to buy more beef. As housewives' demand for beef increases, grocery stores discover that their inventories of meat are being decreased. So, grocery stores will call slaughter houses and ask them to ship more meat. In order to ship more meat to grocery stores, slaughter houses will call cattle raisers and ask them to ship more cattle. However, ranchers might not be able to satisfy this increased demand for cattle. Even in Texas it takes time to breed larger herds. The result is that not enough meat is available at the old price. As the price of meat is bid up, the excess demand for beef is reduced. The average of all prices goes up, and that is inflation. Of course an increase in the price of beef is not offset by a fall in some other prices, because the total demand for goods has risen (everyone has an extra $100).

Suppose now that the same thing happens in the Soviet Union. Everybody has an extra $100 to spend. Grocery stores will discover that they do not have enough beef to satisfy all their customers, so managers will call *planners* and ask them for more beef. Since everything is tightly planned in the Soviet Union, planners will say that all the beef has already been allocated. Now some buyers who like beef a lot might be willing to raise their money offers in order to induce others to give up some beef; however, the price of beef is set by the state and cannot be changed. The Soviet consumer does not have the choice of trying to get more beef by raising his offer. At the old price, the supply of beef is not sufficient to satisfy the increased demand. What can the Soviet consumer do? He can get up early and try to get to the store before others do. But others will do the same thing. A predictable outcome is that a long queue will form in the front of various stores. Those who are *willing* and *able* to wait longer than others will get more beef. Some others might try to work out a deal with the grocer. They might offer to pay *him* some extra money for beef. It is, of course, illegal for the grocer to accept bribes. But it is safe to assume that some do. At any rate, long queues in front of different stores are the predictable consequence of administratively controlled prices.

What is the difference between flexible prices in the United States that translate themselves into inflation whenever our purchasing power exceeds the existing supply of goods, and inflexible prices in the Soviet Union that translate themselves into long queues whenever the people's purchasing power exceeds the supply of goods? When prices go up in the United States, the purchasing power of the consumer's money income is reduced. When stable prices in the USSR create shortages of goods, purchasing power of the consumer's *time* is reduced. Inflation in the USSR reveals inself *via* an increase in the waiting time needed to obtain goods.

Statistical data confirm the Soviet government's emphasis on both economic growth and administrative price controls.[8] The consumer price index in the USSR remained virtually unchanged since 1960. The Soviet Gross National Product (GNP) stood at about 55 percent of the U.S. GNP in the mid-1970s. But its allocations between various uses reflect quite clearly the differences between the command economy of Russia and the free economy of the United States. Total consumption in the USSR is currently slightly over one-third of that in the U.S. At the same time, investment and government expenditures in Russia as percentages of U.S. are about 115 and 63 respectively, well in excess of the ratio of gross national products of the two countries.

---

[8]All data are from *Handbook of Economic Statistics*, Washington, D.C., Office of Economic Research, Central Intelligence Agency, 1976.

Total consumption in the Soviet Union has been about 57 percent of its Gross National Product. That compares to 65 percent in the U.S.A. In addition, the Soviet consumer cannot, via the market place, determine the composition of consumer goods.

Chapter 7

The Soviet Consumer

The Soviet consumer is free to spend his income in any way he chooses. That is, he has a freedom of choice. However, the consumer's freedom of choice is limited to the goods that the planners have decided to produce for him. The consumer's sovereignty, as we know it in the West, does not exist in the Soviet Union. The Soviet consumer cannot affect the composition of output directly.

Consider the American consumer. He is surrounded with a variety of consumer goods. Those goods include pizzas, shoes, cars, houses and chewing gum. Given his income and market prices, the consumer's spending reflects his "likes" and "dislikes". Suppose that, among other things, he wants sausage pizza. He reveals his demand for this particular type of pizza by ordering it. The seller might be able to satisfy the consumer's demand, or he might apologize to him and offer an alternative type of pizza. But the owner will eventually serve it. His own survival depends on making precisely those things that the people want to buy. However, in order to be able to produce sausage pizza he has to purchase all kinds of ingredients and equipment. He will place his orders for those inputs into the production of pizza (e.g., flour, ovens) with other producers. Those people also own their businesses and they want to make money. Once again, the best way for them to make money is to produce ingredients and equipment that their customers want. But, in order to deliver what is demanded they must first produce it. True, they will get their investment plus profit back when the goods are delivered; but they need money now. The producer might have his own money, but it is more likely that he will have to go to either a bank or some other financial institution and ask for a loan. The banks and financial institutions will probably respond and give him credit. Why? Because he is going to produce raw materials and equipment that other people want to buy, something that is in high demand. Thus, he is likely to make profits. And if he is likely to make profits, he is also more likely to be able to pay interest than a producer who wants to produce something that is not in such high demand. In this manner, the consumer goods industry gets from the producers' goods industry what it needs to make pizza with sausage. Finally, and most importantly, the consumer gets what he wants.

It is important to understand the benefits we derive from the system that rests on our freedom of choice, the profit motive, and competition. The system tends not only to produce the kinds of goods that consumers want, but also in the quantities in which people want them. Two economists, Alchian and Allen, put it as follows:

> *Food is grown, harvested, sorted, processed, packed, transported, assembled in appropriately small bundles and offered to consumers every day by individuals pursuing personal interests. No authority is responsible for seeing that these functions are performed and that the right amount of foods is produced. Yet food is available every day. On the other hand, especially appointed authorities are responsible for seeing that such things as water, education and electricity are made available. Is it not paradoxical that in the very areas where we consciously plan and control social output, we often*

> *find shortages and failure of service? References
> to classroom and water shortages are rife; but
> who has heared of a shortage of restaurants,
> churches, beer, shoes or paper? Even further, is
> it now surprising that privately owned business-
> es, operating for the private gain of the owners,
> provide as good, if not better, service to custom-
> ers as do the post office, schools and other pub-
> licly owned enterprises.*[9]

Let us now consider the Soviet consumer. Compared
to the variety of consumer goods that are available to his
American counterpart, the Soviet consumer has fewer
goods from which to choose. Yet he does have the freedom
of choice. Suppose that he also wants to eat pizza with
sausage. Like the American consumer, he reveals his demand for pizza with sausage by asking for it. The seller
might or might not have it. In any case, the seller will relay
information about what people want to the *authorities*.
The seller *cannot* place his order for more sausages and
equipment with the suppliers. He also has no incentives to
do that. The seller's survival depends on fulfillment of the
plan, and is not related to pleasing the consumer. The authorities receive this information. But the planners do not
operate for profit. Compared to the producer in the U.S.,
it is *less* important for the planner to respond to the consumers' preferences. His priorities for the use of resources
are based not on what the consumer is willing to pay, but
on what the leadership wants. Thus the consumer will not
get what he wants; he can only choose from among those
goods that the government decides to produce for him. If
the supply of pizza is less than the consumers' demand for
pizza, there will be shortages. The problem of "who gets

---

[9]Alchian and Allen, *University Economics*, Belmont: Wadsworth Co., 1972, p. 8.

pizza" will be resolved by the first-come, first-served type of competition. Once again, a predictable consequence of the Soviet system of economic planning is long queues for all sorts of consumer goods.

There is one market in the USSR that is similar to what we have in the United States. It is the so-called "collective farm market." This is the market where agricultural products are sold at prices that equate supply and demand. There are two sources of supply for the farm market: The food raised by collective farmers on their individual lots, and the excess supply of the output produced on collective farms over and above their own consumption and compulsory (planned) deliveries to the state. Prices in the farm market are much higher (the ratio of free prices to state prices is about 2.0) than controlled prices in state stores.

The state derives substantial benefits from the existence of farm markets. First, those markets supplement the supply of foods that is available to the population. Second, the farm markets absorb the excess purchasing power. The farm market prices are free to move up. So when there is a shortage of watermelons in state stores, the price of watermelons will not go up — but queues will get longer. The excess of purchasing power is then absorbed in the farm markets where prices are bid up. The potential discrepancy between the people's purchasing power and the supply of consumer goods has always been a major problem for Soviet planners. The Soviet leadership is caught between two political needs. On the one hand, it is desirable for the rulers to raise the standard of living of those over whom they rule. On the other hand, the development of heavy industries is perceived by Soviet leaders to be a major vehicle for the expansion of their power, both domestically and internationally. In order to eliminate the excess purchasing power, Soviet planners try to set prices of consumer goods in such a way that the total value of all consumer goods approximates the sum total of wages. Suppose that wages paid out to Soviet workers are figured to be $1,000,000, and that the plan calls for the production of 10,000 units of consumer goods. The government then sets an average price per unit of consumer goods at $100. As long as the Soviet people were willing to purchase all that was produced, the excess purchasing power was not a major problem. However, improvements in the standard of living in the late 1960's and early 1970's affected the Soviet consumer. Instead of just grabbing anything in sight, he started looking around for some of the better things in life. Unfortunately for the consumer, the performance of Soviet firms is judged by their ability to meet output targets, and their managers are rewarded for the quantities of goods they produce. The result is that the Soviet consumer today does not buy everything that he finds in stores. One can find many references to this problem in the Soviet press. For example, it was reported that sales of clothing and underwear were falling 50 percent behind the growth of unsold inventory. This accumulation of unsold goods means that the Soviet consumer is not spending his entire income. It also means that queues for goods that he likes are getting longer and that the scope of black market activities for good "stuff" is likely to expand. None of those things is liked by the leadership.

In comparison with the American consumer, the Soviet citizen consumes about one-third the goods and services. At the same time, GNP in the USSR is about 55 percent of that in the U.S. Some interesting statistics are shown in Figure 7.

Figure 7

U.S.S.R.—U.S.

Per Capita Consumption, 1973

Consumption Goods	U.S.S.R. as a percent of U.S.
Education	64
Health	34
Personal Services	31
Durable Goods	8
Soft Goods	20
Food	62
Total Consumption:	34

Source: *Allocation of Resources in the Soviet Union and China;* Washington, D.C.: Joint Economic Committee, Congress of the U.S., 1975, p. 19.

In 1979, total grain production per person in the USSR stood at 94 percent of U.S., meat production per person was 74 percent, the number of television receivers in use per thousand persons was 37 percent, and so on.

The average monthly wage of the Soviet worker in January 1979 was about 161 rubles (approximately $243 at the Soviet official exchange rate). According to Soviet calculations, the minimum acceptable standard of living for a family of three requires an income of 155 rubles per month. Low average earnings in relation to the standard of living requirements explain the high percentage of women participating in the Soviet labor force. The Soviet labor force is about 56 percent of the total population. In the United States about 47 percent of the population is included in the labor force. The agricalatural labor force in the USSR is 13 percent of its total population (2 percent in the U.S.).

The minimum wage in the Soviet Union was set at 70 rubles per week in the mid-1970s. What could 70 rubles buy in Russia? Here are some prices from Leningrad stores: nylon stockings cost 7 rubles, a slip is 40-50 rubles, men's pajamas are about 70 rubles, and meat costs about 3-4 rubles per kilogram (two pounds). Bread in Russia is delicious and inexpensive (about .30 rubles per kilogram). Prices in the farm markets are much higher than in state stores. One watermelon costs about 7 rubles, which means that a person receiving 70 rubles could buy about 7 watermelons per month.

It is always difficult to compare prices in different countries because they all use different currencies. One method for comparing the standard of living in different countries is to ask: How long does an average worker have to work in order to purchase various consumer goods? Figure 8 shows the number of hours of work by average wage earners in Moscow and Washington, D.C. that were required in March of 1979 for the purchase of different goods. London is also included to give perspective to the comparison. It understates *real* prices of goods in the USSR because the *cost of waiting* in line for goods is not included in the comparison.

Figure 8
Comparative Standard Of Living

Approximate worktime required for average manufacturing employee to buy selected commodities in retail stores in Washington, D.C., and London, and at state-fixed prices in Moscow during March 1979. (London is included for perspective.)

Commodity	Wash. D.C.	London	Moscow
Milk (1 liter)	7 min.	9 min.	18 min.
Hamburger meat, beef (1 kg)	43 min.	57 min.	128 min.
Potatoes (1 kg)	2 min.	4 min.	7 min.

Apples, eating (1 kg)	11 min.	15 min.	40 min.
Sugar (1 kg)	5 min.	11 min.	59 min.
White bread (1 kg)	8 min.	12 min.	18 min.
Eggs (1 dz)	12 min.	24 min.	99 min.
Vodka (0.5 liter)	52 min.	161 min.	380 min.
Cigarettes (20)	9 min.	22 min.	23 min.
Weekly food basket (for 4)	12.5 hr.	21.4 hr.	42.3 hr.
Soap, toilet (150 grams)	5 min.	6 min.	23 min.
Lipstick	26 min.	50 min.	72 min.
Panty hose	22 min.	11 min.	427 min.
Men's leather shoes	8 hr.	11 hr.	33 hr.
Man's business suit	20 hr.	25 hr.	68 hr.
Refrigerator, small (120 liters)	43 hr.	35 hr.	208 hr.

Source: "Keith Bush, *Retail Prices in Moscow and Four Western Cities in March 1979,* Radio Liberty Research Munich, Germany. Worktime is based on average take-home pay of male and female manufacturing workers. Income taxes, Social Security taxes (U.S. and U.K.), health insurance premiums (U.S. and U.K.) and unemployment insurance (U.K. only) have been deducted from wages: family allowances (U.K. and U.S.S.R.) have been added for a family of four in dollars, hourly take-home pay in January 1979 was $4.61 for American workers, $3.25 for British workers and $1.38 for Russian workers.

Some items, such as lipstick and panty hose, could not be found by any surveyor in Moscow in any state retail store at the time of the survey. The price given is that seen in the past.

Money wage differentials exist in the Soviet Union. The span between the average highest income and the average lowest income is 1:3:5. However, these are averages. Directors of large enterprises, high officials and top scientists earn more than 1,000 rubles a month. Compared to the minimum wage of 70 rubles, that is a big salary. Moreover, the wage differential does not fully explain the difference between income groups in the Soviet Union. Upper income groups (high Party and government officials, high-ranking military personnel, scientists, engineers, managers of enterprises) have access to "special stores" where they can buy goods that are not available to ordinary Russians. Effectively, prices paid by the richest and most powerful are reduced by the average cost of waiting for goods in front of state stores. They also receive a number of valuable benefits such as better housing, a summer house, an official car, etc. If we include those things into our measure of income distribution in the Soviet Union, the observed money income differential between the upper and lower income groups is, in fact, much larger. Figure 9 provides information on the distribution of income by families in a region (unspecified) of the Soviet Union in 1970.

Figure 9
Families of Workers and Employees
By Annual Income

Monthly Income Per Person In Rubles	Percentage of Total Number of Wage Earners
less than 50	32.6
51-75	31.2
76-100	17.7
101-125	9.1
126-175	7.1
more than 176	2.3

Source: Korzhenevskiy, *Osnovnyye,* 1971, p. 112.

It is clear from this table that incomes are unequal in the Soviet Union. It is also clear that the majority of people in the country earn no more than the minimum wage. Members of collective farms, who are among the poorest people in the USSR, receive a part of their compensation *in kind.* Their money wages are below the minimum wage.

Chapter 8

The Soviet Firm

The position of the Soviet manager differs considerably from that of his counterpart in the United States. In theory, he has no decision-making powers of any consequence. His job is to inform the planners about his plant's production possibilities and the requirements for raw materials, intermediary goods, capital equipment and labor. The manager then receives the firm's production and supply plans and is responsible for carrying them out. To encourage the manager to fulfill the firm's plan, his income is supplemented with bonuses for above-plan performance. The Soviet manager's tenure on the job, promotions and income (including privileges that go with his position) depend on his ability to produce *at least* the planned output quota. If and when he does better than that, his income, prestige and standing with the officials are bound to improve.

In practice, the Soviet manager can create for himself some decision-making powers. Actually he finds it in his self-interest to do so. The relevant question is *how* and *why* the manager can transfer decision-making powers from the state to himself. Most importantly, the answer to this question will explain the puzzling dilemma we noted earlier in this book; how and why the Soviet economy can experience economic gains in an environment which is admittedly ridden with waste and inefficiencies.

To ensure his survival on the job, the manager understates the production capacities of the firm. In this way he makes the task of producing his output quota much easier. The planners know this, but there is little they can do about it. It would be impossible for them to check the accuracy of each and every report they receive from managers. Moreover, the Soviet manager knows that the planned supplies that he needs are frequently delivered late, or not at all, or in the wrong quantities. True, the manager can justify his lack of performance by explaining to the authorities that his planned supplies did not arrive in time. However, he can do better for himself by fulfilling the plan anyhow. So when he submits his requests for raw materials, intermediary goods and labor, the Soviet manager always overstates his needs. He wants to accumulate those supplies to obviate production crises. The result is that the manager, moved by his own survival trait, creates for himself a set of opportunity choices that are in direct violation of the intent of the Soviet system of economic planning.

Given the firm's *true* production capacities, the manager can then choose to produce no more than his output quota. In that case, the manager will have some supplies left over for future emergencies. However, he will also forego the rewards he could receive for overfulfillment of the plan. The manager can also choose to overfulfill his output quota. In that case, the manager will get a bonus; but he will also use up the allocated supplies. The greater the probability of late deliveries of the planned supplies, the more importance the manager is likely to attach to the accumulation of unreported stocks.

The unreported stocks permit the firm to meet its output quota and produce an output stream considered desirable by the state. Thus, the existence of the firm's unplanned inventories reduces the effects of waste and inefficiencies in the Soviet system of administrative planning.

The so-called "Schekino experiment" clearly illustrates the Soviet manager's response to the Soviet system of incentives. In 1967, the Schekino Chemical Combine was designed by the state as a laboratory for testing new economic concepts. The factory received the target of increasing output by 80 percent by the end of 1970, while its Wage Fund was frozen at the 1967 level. Given the Wage Fund, the average wage was then tied to the level of employment. A fall in the size of the labor force meant an increase in the average wage for those remaining with the force. By the end of 1969 the firm's output target was attained, labor productivity had grown by 107 percent, and the management reported that the labor force was reduced from 8,000 to 7,000 workers. [10] This phenomenal increase in labor productivity can be explained as follows: The firm held an unreported inventory of labor in 1967; that is, the firm could have traded this inventory for additional output in that year but chose not to do so. The firm was then handed a new system of rewards, and the manager found himself in a new and different position. The excess of labor turned from an asset into a liability. The manager's only rational decision was to economize on the use of labor. The result was then revealed to the state as a jump in the *reported* productivity of labor.

The difference between the approved and reported production capacities enables the Soviet manager to accumulate stocks essential for his survival. However, his ability to accumulate stocks is limited only to those supplies he *actually* receives. Suppose the manager of a firm needs only two inputs, A and B. The plan promises to the firm 100 units fo A and 100 Units of B. The manager needs, say, 80 units of A and 70 units of B in order to produce the planned output target. The firm also receives its quota of A (100) on time. The function of this surplus of twenty units of A

[10] K. Bush, "The Implementation of the Soviet Economic Reform," unpublished paper, pp. 30-34.

is to create for the manager a set of opportunity choices between higher output and current income on the one hand, and security against future emergencies on the other. But what if the firm receives less than the entire allocation of B so that its total supply of B (including reserves) is not sufficient to cover the deficit. It then appears that the ability of the Soviet manager to accumulate stocks *via* false reporting to the state is a necessary (but certainly not a sufficient) condition for fulfilling the plan.

The manager who does not get his allotment of B can eventually explain his short-fall to the authorities. However, the manager can do much better for himself if he somehow delivers the required output on time. The manager will therefore view his reserve of supplies in a new and different light. In addition to providing the manager with security against future shortcomings in the system of planning, the unreported stocks are also his source of purchasing power. The manager trades those stocks with other managers in what has come to be known as "informal markets." True, the cost of information about exchange opportunities is greater, and the extent of exchange less, than what it would be if the manager could use cash. It would be much simpler for the manager to sell his surplus of A to whoever is short of it, and then use the proceeds from the sale to purchase B. As we recall from our discussion of the Soviet system of planning, the Soviet firm cannot hold cash balances — all cash must be turned over to the bank. Consequently, the Soviet manager who has a surplus of A and needs B must seek someone who has B and needs A. The extent of exchange is then impeded. However, as long as some trade occurs, resources move towards higher-valued uses. This is yet another reason why the Soviet manager, acting in his own self-interest, reduces waste and inefficiencies in the Soviet plan. In fact, those informal markets save the Soviet system of administrative planning from breakdown.

The long-term consequences of overfulfillment of quotas present a clear danger to the Soviet manager. Each time he overfulfills his quota the state is likely to give him a new and higher output target for the next period. A revised production target reduces, in turn, his range of opportunity choices.

As long as the Soviet manager views the existence of his discretionary range of choices as an essential survival requirement, he will be eager to preserve it. In reality, it means that he must *raise* the firm's productivity and *conceal* it from the state in order to offset the effect of a revised production target on his area of discretion. It follows that the Soviet system has a built-in incentive for the manager to search for cost-saving improvements, providing the manager can choose the rate at which the effects of these improvements are made known to the state.

It is important to note that the manager's incentive to generate and promote innovative behavior benefits the economy as a whole. The extent of this activity is an empirical question. It is also a very difficult one to investigate. Nevertheless, Soviet reality strongly suggests the existence of some innovative behavior by managers. How else would one explain the fact that, after so many years of central planning, the Soviet manager has preserved his discretionary range of choices and is still able to trade current output for additional reserves of supplies.

Each time the Soviet manager engages in "informal" activities, he reduces waste and inefficiences in the Soviet economy. The important point is that the fulfillment of the Soviet plan depends, at least in part, on the manager's ability to violate the government's own laws and regulations. That is, the attainment of the ruling group's objectives depends on its willingness to accept some illegal reallocation of decision-making powers between the state and the firm in favor of the latter.

Chapter 9

Soviet Agriculture

Soviet agriculture is backward in comparison with both Soviet industry and American agriculture. Agricultural sectors in the USSR account for more than one-fifth of the Soviet Gross National Product, and employ almost one-third of the labor force. In comparison, the agricultural sector in the U.S. contributes about 3-4 percent of its Gross National Product and employs 5 percent of the labor force. The Soviet Union has yet to produce the quantity and quality of foodstuffs desired by its population. The average output produced by a Soviet farmer is about 10 percent of the U.S. average.

The performance of Soviet agriculture — or the lack of it — is usually attributed to bad weather, low priority for investment funds and the lack of incentives. As I read the Soviet evidence, the last item is perhaps the most critical. For there is one sector in the Soviet agriculture that has not failed to perform well in spite of bad weather and a low rate of investment. It is the so-called "private sector".

It is not argued here that the rate of investment in Soviet agriculture is of no consequence. Indeed, it is. The issue is one of assessing the relative importance of various factors that have contributed to the performance of Soviet agriculture.

The Soviet economic plan for agriculture always promises to increase investment in machinery and equipment. It always has consistently failed to fulfill that promise. We know the major reason for this failure. The plan is far from being perfect. So, as planning mistakes are revealed, the government has to make numerous corrections and changes in the plan. Those changes are always made at the expense of low-priority sectors like agriculture. For example, the plan for 1966-1970 specified that 1,790,000 tractors must be produced and delivered to the agricultural sector. It turned out that less than 1,500,000 tractors were produced during that period. In one area alone (Poltava Oblast) in 1968, the planned deliveries were met to the following extent: tractors 58 percent, combines 61 percent, trucks 28 percent, milking machines 18 percent, and plows 10 percent.

To understand the system of incentives in the USSR it is necessary to explain the organization of Soviet agriculture. It consists of three sectors: state farms, collective farms, and private plots.

The main productive unit of the state sector is the *Sovkhoz*. The Sovkhoz is governed by the same rules that apply to other state enterprises, and has its production and financial plan like any other firm in Russia. Its employees, however, are paid a wage that is not strongly linked to their performance. In the early 1970's there were about 15,000 state farms in Russia. They made up about half the total agricultural area in the Soviet Union.

The main productive unit of the collective sector is the *Kolkhoz*. There were about 33,000 collectives in the early 1970's. The average Kolkhoz has about 15,000 acres, about 450 households, some 60 tractors, 1,300 cattle and 1,600 sheep and goats. In theory, the major differences between the Sovkhoz and Kolkhoz are: collective, as opposed to state, ownership; and elected, as opposed to appointed, management. Given the overall control by the Party officials, those differences do not really matter.

The Kolkhoz has to deliver a predetermined quota of its output to the state at low prices. It is really a tax *in kind*. What is left after the tax is shared by the collective farmers in accordance with the number of days each of them spent in the fields. Some of the output is consumed directly by members and some is sold in farm markets, with the proceeds shared by collective farmers. Thus, the total income of collective farmers consists of payments *in kind* and monetary compensation. In general, farmers' incomes are below the average earnings of industrial workers.

The private sector consists of household subsidiary plots (about an acre per household) and household livestock holdings. Both collective and state farms' households are entitled to such plots. They do not have the right of ownership in that land — just the right to use it. On those plots households can grow anything they want for their own consumption or to be offered for sale in collective farm markets. They are also entitled to have a cow, two pigs and as many chickens as they want. Those plots account for about *three percent of the total agricultural area* in the Soviet Union. Yet, they make a significant contribution to the total output in agriculture. This private sector contributes *65 percent of the total output of potatoes, 40 percent of the total output of vegetables, 35 percent of the total output of milk and meat*, and *50 percent of the total output of eggs*. In general, the *private sector provides about thirty three percent of the total agricultural output in the USSR.*

On the average, private lots supply about 44 percent of the total income in cash and kind received by collective farm families. This explains why the government tolerates the private sector. As bad as their agricultural situation is, it would be much worse in the absence of the private sector. In fact, the performance of the private sector indicates that the major cause of agricultural problems in the USSR is the lack of incentives.

Chapter 10

Concluding Remarks

In the mid 1960's the Soviet Union began to feel strong pressures to substitute economic relations for rigid administrative planning. The "economic reforms," as those pressures got to be called, were suggestive of a change in the Communist belief that administrative planning is superior to the market-oriented allocation of resources. The real purpose of economic reforms was, then, to search for a set of institutions which would (i) preserve the general characteristics of the system, (ii) provide for the same or better performance of the economy, and (iii) reduce the rather unpleasant and embarrassing dependence of the economy and the ruling group on illegal activities of Soviet managers.

The purpose of economic reforms in the USSR was to create a greater scope of freedom for the manager in pursuing innovating activities, and develop adequate incentives to economize on the use of labor, capital and other resources. Those changes in the behavior of the Soviet manager were to be accomplished by relating his rewards to the firm's profits, production costs, and its stock of capital.

Soviet economic reforms never had much of a chance. The Soviet bureaucracy lost no time in stalling these reforms. By the early 1970's, economic reforms were largely out and the old system of planning was continued. And so were the old problems. R. Bush wrote:

> *Early in 1970, one plant director wrote of two years' delay in obtaining certain material inputs, while another director dwelt bitterly on the lack of supplies. Over 40,000 basic producer goods are still administratively allocated . . . if the rates of recruitment achieved in 1966 and 1967 are maintained, the material-technical branch will have grown by 250,000-300,000 functionaries during the Eighth Five-Year Plan.*[11]

And G. Schroeder said:

> *Although there is still much talk in the Soviet press about economic reforms, the phrase now has come to mean simply all changes in economic management procedures that are made to improve the existing systems. There is little mention of spontaneity, except to condemn it, or for granting more decision-making authority to enterprises.*[12]

Soviet rulers have come to depend on their bureaucracy for running the state as well as for controlling the population. The bureaucracy, in turn, finds deviations from the systems of administrative planning contrary to its self-interest. Thus, economic reforms in the Soviet Union are likely to be talked about — for the system needs improvements — but they stand no prayer of being implemented unless there is a major change in the balance of power in that country. In the meantime, the Soviet consumer will continue to be a major victim of the system.

[11]K. Bush, "The Implementations of the Soviet Economic Reforms," Unpublished paper, pp. 29-30.

[12]G. Schroeder, "Recent Developments in Soviet Planning and Incentives," in *Soviet Economic Perspectives for the Seventies*, pp. 35-36.

A major benefactor from budgetary allocation in the Soviet Union is that country's military establishment. While the overall rate of economic growth in the Soviet Union has been slowing in the 1960's and 1970's for reasons explained in Chapter 25, Soviet defense programs have maintained a steady growth.

Since the Soviet Union is our major adversary, it is important to have some understanding of its spending for national defense. The description of Soviet defense programs in Appendix I shows that recent economic problems in Russia are causing no major changes in that country's defense policy. The picture that emerges from Appendix I shows that the Soviet government is willing to impose a very high price on its people in order to further its imperialistic goals.

APPENDIX I
SOVIET DEFENSE SPENDING

Compared to a wealth of statistical data that are available in the West, Soviet statistics are sparse, incomplete and not very reliable. This is especially true of statistics on Soviet defense spending. Working through Soviet data on military expenditures is like doing a crossword puzzle. There is a general consensus among American experts on the Soviet affairs that our estimates of the costs of Soviet defense spending could be in error by as much as 15 percent.

Estimated Soviet spending for defense increased from over 40 billion rubles in 1967 to over 58 billion rubles in 1977. Of course, those are figured in *constant* rubles, because Soviet prices have remained stable throughout the period. As a percentage of their GNP, Soviet military expenditures are about 12 percent. In the U.S.A., defense spending accounts for about 10 percent of the GNP.

Soviet defense expenditures have been rising at a real annual growth rate of about 3-4 percent. U.S. defense outlays in *constant* dollars have been falling since 1972. In addition, the Soviet military has the first pick of scientific, technical and skilled workers.

Major categories of Soviet military expenditures are investment, operating expenditures, and research and development. Investment includes spending for new equipment and facilities. Investment expenditures, which reflect the flow of new weapons systems, averaged about one-half of Soviet defense spending. Operating expenditures are for maintaining current forces. Those include personnel costs, operation and maintenance expenditures, and account for over one-quarter of Soviet defense spending. The estimate for Soviet research and development outlays is the hardest to obtain. Thus, our estimate of Soviet expenditures in new technology and ideas is quite likely to be less reliable than the estimates of investment and operating expenditures. Western experts believe that nearly one-fourth of Soviet defense spending is earmarked for exploring new technologies and improving existing weapons.

Three sets of Soviet armed forces that are of concern to public decision-makers in the U.S.A. are: inter-continental attack forces, the tactical air and ground forces in Eastern Europe, and the armed forces along the China border. Priorities that the Soviet govement assigns to those three sets of forces disclose something about Soviet hopes and aspirations for the future. Intercontinental attack forces are allocated about 10 percent of their total defense spending. Soviet forces in Eastern Europe get less than 10 percent of total spending, and the Soviet forces along the Sino-Soviet border account for a little over 10 percent of total spending. Moreover, their rate of growth has exceeded that of defense spending as a whole.

It is safe to assume that the Soviet defense establishment will continue to enjoy top priority in the USSR. Defense spending has been growing in real terms, and defense activities have been well funded. The Soviet leaders are certainly concerned about gloomy economic prospects. Yet, it would be wrong to assume that present and future economic problems in the Soviet Union will bring about major changes in defense policy.

Figure I

US and Soviet Investment and Operating, 1966-1976

A Comparison of US Outlays and Estimated Dollar Costs of the Soviet Activities if Duplicated in the US

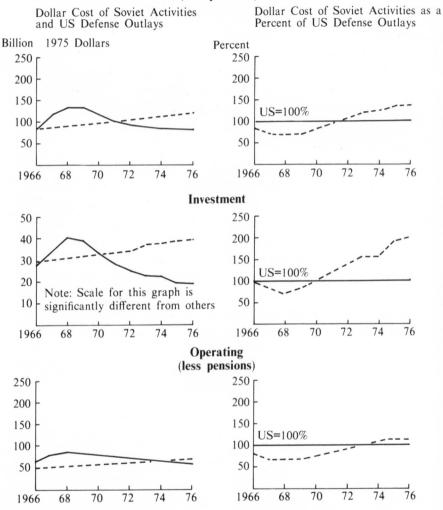

Total Defense Costs
(less pensions)

Dollar Cost of Soviet Activities and US Defense Outlays

Dollar Cost of Soviet Activities as a Percent of US Defense Outlays

Billion 1975 Dollars

Percent

US=100%

Investment

Note: Scale for this graph is significantly different from others

US=100%

Operating
(less pensions)

US=100%

Cumulative 1966-76

| US | Investment | Operating | 1025 |
| USSR | Investment | Operating | 1005 |

Investment includes all costs for procurement of military hardware and for the construction of facilities, but excludes RDT&E. Operating includes all personnel-related costs (with the exception of pensions) and all costs associated with the operation and maintenance of weapon systems and equipment.

The following books are available from The Fisher Institute

QUANTITY   TOTAL PRICE

_____ copy of FUNDAMENTALS OF ECONOMICS: A
PROPERTY RIGHTS APPROACH by Dr. Svetozar
Pejovich (Fisher Institute). The inclusion of new property rights concepts updates the field of economics in
this basic textbook for beginning business/economics
students and educated laymen. 258 pages, 51 charts and
tables.

$11.95 (hardback) _____

_____ copy of TAX LIMITATION, INFLATION & THE
ROLE OF GOVERNMENT by Milton Friedman
(Fisher Institute). The Nobel Laureate has been called
the most influential economist of this era. This new book
will give you a broad picture of economic research and
a fascinating overview of free market philosophy. It is
sound public policy material. 110 pages, 15 graphs, 2
tables.

$5.95 (paperback); $9.95 (hardback) _____

_____ copy of THE NEW PROTECTIONISM: The Welfare
State & International Trade by Melvyn B. Krauss (International Center for Economic Policy Studies). Professor Krauss presents a clear and essentially non-
technical discussion of trade theory and policy in defense of free trade. 117 pages, 5 charts.

$3.95 (paperback) _____

_____ copy of FISHER'S CONCISE HISTORY OF ECO-
NOMIC BUNGLING by Antony Fisher (Caroline
House). Fisher uses 5,000 years of economic history,
logic, wit, anecdote, and a keen understanding to show
how the free market system works best to improve every
citizen's economic well-being. 113 pages of facinating
reading.

_____ $2.95 (paperback) _____

Please add $1.00 **PER BOOK** for postage & handling .... $_____
(Plus 50¢ per book state tax if buyer resides in Texas)

Enclosed is my payment in full of .... $_____

Name_____

Title_____Company_____

Address_____

City_____State_____Zip_____

*Please send information about the Fisher Institute ☐